Elizabeth J. Thompson - 2497

W9-CBC-079

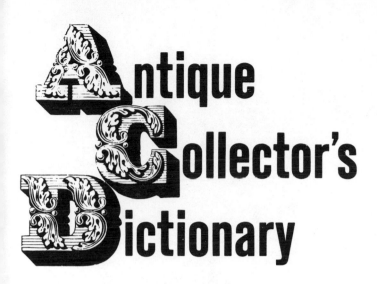

Antique Collector's Dictionary

Donald Cowie and Keith Henshaw

GRAMERCY PUBLISHING COMPANY • NEW YORK

Copyright © Donald Cowie and Keith Henshaw, MCMLXII
All Rights Reserved
Library of Congress Catalog Number 62-21523
Printed in U.S.A.

This edition published by Gramercy Publishing Company,
a division of Crown Publishers, Inc.,
by arrangement with Arco Publishing Co., Inc.

g h

INTRODUCTION

—

AN introduction to an Antiques Dictionary of this size must be in the nature of an apology for all that has had to be omitted. The compilers found that they could have gone on and on— and on. The amount of discarded material would have filled another volume.

What to retain and what to discard, that was the question. Often, the answer had to be arbitrary. But a great deal remains: furniture, ceramics, glass, silver, clocks, carpets, tapestries, metalware, etc., forms of decoration, styles, the men who fashioned the wares and created the styles, and then the thousand-and-one words seemingly coined to vex us—almery, amboyna, amphora, andiron, *an hua*. . . .

The other problem was that of emphasis. The following example shows how the problem has been solved, or rather, dealt with: Sèvres porcelain is more important than Derby, and the wares produced at the Chinese Imperial Factories of Ching-tê-Chên are more important than either; but Derby receives the longest entry because *this work is primarily intended for the American (and British) reader*.

For the rest, inquire within.

ANTIQUE COLLECTORS' DICTIONARY

Abbey, Richard Liverpool potter, apprenticed to Sadler & Green; founded the Herculaneum (q.v.) factory *c*. 1793.

Abbotsford Furniture Victorian Gothick, from 1830's, dark oak usually, or walnut; the chair, heavily carved, upholstered in velvet or tapestry, like a Jacobean throne. Vogue attributed to Scott's novels. (Sometimes called 'Baronial'.)

Acacia A decorative wood that shows a contrast between the pale yellow sapwood and the dark heartwood. The false-acacia or locust-tree (*Robinia pseudo-acacia*) was introduced into England during the seventeenth century.

Acanthus Ornament derived from the stylized foliage of the acanthus on Greek and Roman decoration, as dandelion leaf; much favoured by the Chippendale school.

Acier, Michael-Victor Porcelain modeller (a Frenchman) who was installed in 1764 as chief modeller at Meissen, jointly with Kändler, a post he held until 1779.

Adam, Robert (1728–92) Distinguished architect and designer who was responsible, more than any other one person, for the introduction of a classical revival in England. In their *Works in Architecture*, by Robert and his brother James Adam, which began to come out in 1773, they claimed to have brought about 'a kind of Revolution in the whole System' of architecture. The Adam style in furniture, and ceramics, is characterized by severe classical motifs. The Adams made no furniture themselves.

Adams A famous and recurring name in Staffordshire. The most important are three William Adams. The first (1746–1805) made at Burslem from about 1770 and at Tunstall from about

*Examples of Adam
furniture*

Bookcase

Chair

Table

8

1780 cream-coloured earthenware, blue-printed earthenware and, most notably, jasper ware that rivalled that of Wedgwood. The second (1748–1831) made at Cobridge and at Burslem from about 1770 various kinds of earthenware and, in the early nineteenth century, some china. The third (1772–1829) was in partnership with his father-in-law at Burslem for a time, but from 1804 was in business on his own at Stoke-on-Trent, making useful earthenware and stoneware, bone china (from *c.* 1810) and Parian statuary. The business was carried on by his several sons until 1864.

Adams and Adams-Deane Revolver   Patented by Webley and Robert Adams in 1851, this was England's answer to the Colt (q.v.) from which it differed by being a double-action piece and by being stronger and faster, but less accurate at long range and the parts were not interchangeable.

Agate Ware   Pottery in which clays of different colours are kneaded together in imitation of veined agate.

Air-twist Glass Stems   An English glass-making development that dates from about 1735. Air bubbles were let into the thick base of the bowl and the base was drawn down and twisted into a stem, the elongated bubbles thus forming corkscrew air lines inside the stem. In later examples the stem was made separately, still on the principle of the extended air bubble, being cut from long lengths; later again, from about 1750, a moulded process brought with it much greater uniformity in the spiral and allowed for compound twists of considerable variety.

Albarello   Waisted, cylindrical drug jar.

Alcora   A faience factory founded in this Spanish town in the Province of Valencia about 1727, the wares produced being in the style of Moustiers (q.v.) until the 1780's, when the factory turned to the manufacture of creamwares in the English manner.

Alder Wood used in the eighteenth century for country furniture; white with pinkish tinge, usually marked with knots and curls.

Alloy Combination of metals fused together; a base metal mixed with a precious one to make it workable, to harden it, to change its colour.

Almery A cupboard in a wall or piece of furniture; a safe for food; a press for clothing and other objects; a doored recess in a church for the storing of sacred utensils. (Also called ambry, *aumbry*.)

Amberina Translucent flint glass, often with air bubbles, shading red to amber.

Amboyna Name given to certain burr woods imported from the Moluccas and Borneo; brown with yellow tinge and marked with small knots and curls. Also a West Indian wood similarly marked. Used as a veneer and for inlays and banding.

Amphora Two-handled vessel used by the Greeks and Romans; tall, slender, narrow-necked.

Anatolian Rugs Bright-coloured, often of silk, from Anatolian plateau; woollen warp with two to four coloured wool weft threads between knots; border of one to three stripes; coarse weave owing to fifty to seventy Ghiordiz knots to the square inch.

Andirons Articles of chimney furniture comprising an upright standard on a base or short spread feet, and a horizontal bar, one end of which is affixed to the standard (low down), the other end turning down to form a foot. Andirons (or fire-dogs) belong in a fireplace for which the fuel was wood. Examples survive from the fifteenth century. Most andirons of the sixteenth and seventeenth centuries were of cast iron, but wrought iron specimens are to be met with, while brass, latten and even silver were used from the mid-seventeenth century. With the general use of coal and the grate in the eighteenth century, the andiron went out of use.

An Hua (Chinese) The so-called 'secret' decoration on Chinese porcelain; first used early in the Ming period, perhaps as early as A.D. 1400. This decoration can only be seen when the piece is held up to a light. In some cases the design was engraved on the body with a needle before glazing; in other cases the design was painted in white slip on a white body before glazing.

Anthemium Honeysuckle ornament of classical origin which, understandably, found favour with those who brought about the classical revival in Europe. Its popularity in England lasted well into the Regency period.

Antique A man-made object which should be of manageable proportions, have decorative properties, be more than 100 years old, and which, by reason of its quality, beauty, rarity, antiquity, curiosity, or vogue, is sufficiently esteemed and/or coveted as to have value.

Apostle Spoons Early spoons made in sets of 12, each one surmounted by a different apostle as a knop. Some sets of 13 were made to include the figure of the 'Master' (Christ). 1478 is the earliest hall-mark recorded.

Applewood Hard, fine-grained wood used for country furniture in the eighteenth century; it was also employed for inlay and veneer.

Apron Masking piece under the front edge of a table or seat.

Arabesque Ornament of capricious character: fanciful figures, monsters, fruit and flowers grouped or combined. Used in inlay and marquetry and sometimes in painted Georgian furniture.

Arbor   Horological term for the shafts, axles or spindles of a clock.

Arcanist   Person knowing or claiming to know a secret, especially the secret of porcelain-making.

Argil   Clay, especially potter's clay.

Argyle   A vessel, often of silver, for keeping gravy warm, the actual pot fitting inside an outer container which held hot water. Late Georgian.

Arita   Japanese porcelain made at Arita in the province of Hizen where porcelain has been manufactured since the first half of the sixteenth century. There are two well-known types of decoration, Imari (q.v.) and Kakiemon (q.v.); and as regards shapes, typical are the square, octagonal and hexagonal section vases, which were to be copied by European factories. Arita porcelains began to reach Europe in the second half of the seventeenth century.

Ark   Medieval term for a chest with gabled or canted lid.

Armada Chest   Heavy iron coffer imported from Germany in the late seventeenth and throughout the eighteenth century. The Spanish Armada has nothing to do with this chest, which was the forerunner of the safe.

Armoire   A large cupboard usually enclosed by doors from top to base; parent of the wardrobe.

Armorial China   Chinese porcelain, usually services, painted with coats-of-arms, crests, or initials, made to order for the European market. An increasing amount of such wares were imported into England in the late seventeenth and eighteenth centuries. Some English factories, notably Worcester, made armorial china in the second half of the eighteenth century.

Armour Protective clothing intended to be worn in battle. Mail (small, linked metal rings) was favoured until the early fifteenth century, when the full suit of plate armour came in; this heavy suit began to grow lighter and lighter during the sixteenth century, and though the helmet and the breast plate were considered useful even until the early eighteenth century, most armour from the late sixteenth century onwards was made for ceremonial purposes. (The helmet, of course, is still in use.)

The parts of a full suit of plate armour are as follows. *Helm* or *Helmet* comprising the *skull* (top and back), the *visor* (hinged, to protect eyes and upper face), the *beaver* (often hinged, to protect mouth and lower face). *Gorget* protects the neck and is often articulated. *Pauldron* covers the shoulder joint where body and arm-piece meet (also called *Epaulière*, whence *epaulette* derives). The upper arm is covered by the *Rerebrace*, the elbow by the *Coudière*, the forearm by the *Vambrace* and the hand by the *Gauntlet*. The function of *Breastplate* and *Backplate* are obvious. *Taces* or *Tassets* are the metal strips that make a short skirt to protect the belly. The *Guisse* covers the thigh, the *Genouillère* covers the knee-cap, the *Jamb* covers the lower leg, and the flexible, long-toed shoe is a *Solleret*.

Arquebus The term is loosely used but should be confined to the earliest (fifteenth and sixteenth century) long-arm gun fitted with matchlock and shoulder-butt; of German origin.

Arras From the fourteenth to the sixteenth century Arras, in the Pas de Calais, France, was so famous for its tapestries that the name of the town was applied to a piece of tapestry regardless of where it was made.

Ash A tough, elastic wood, white in colour, veined with streaks in the direction of its growth; used chiefly for seat furniture.

Aspergillum Brush or rod for sprinkling holy water.

Astbury, John and Thomas John Astbury (died 1743), Staffordshire potter whose name is associated with a red earthenware with relief decoration in white clay, also with an improved white ware containing flint in its body. But this improvement is also attributed to John's son, Thomas, who in 1725 set up a factory at Fenton.

Astragal (1) A small convex moulding used between the capital and shaft of the classic order (with the exception of the Greek Doric), and in various positions in later architecture. (2) A bar containing the panes of glass of a window or of a glazed cupboard or bookcase.

Astrolabe Early instrument for taking altitudes and for making astronomical measurements.

Aubusson Famous French centre for carpets and tapestries from the seventeenth century. The tapestries woven here were technically inferior to those of Beauvais and Gobelins; pastoral designs are notable, as are hunting scenes, religious subjects. Most of the Aubusson carpets one sees today are woven wool and without pile and are nineteenth-century products.

Automatic Weapons Date from the 1880's: the Spanish Orbea revolver of 1883, the Maxim machine-gun of 1884, the British Paulson revolver of 1886.

Aventurine Opaque brown Venetian glass, its surface spangled with small pieces of metal. *Also*: a term applied to small fragments of gold wire sprinkled over the surface of lacquer.

Axminster Carpets Carpet weaving begun at Axminster by Thomas Whitley, a cloth weaver, in 1755. He made carpets knotted in the Turkish manner. In 1779 there was 'a considerable manufacture' at Axminster. The factory closed in 1835, the looms being taken to Wilton.

Backgammon Boards More ornamental than chess boards;

14

inlay examples from the seventeenth century are sometimes to be encountered, usually in walnut and oak. Some such boards were incorporated in gaming tables.

Back Stool   A stool with a back in the late sixteenth and first half of the seventeenth century; but in the latter half of the seventeenth and throughout the eighteenth century the term was used to describe a single armless chair.

Baker Rifle   Iron-ramrod-and-mallet muzzle-loader made by the London gunsmith Ezekiel Baker and used by the British Rifle Brigade in the Napoleonic Wars.

Baku Rugs   Of the Caucasian group, the favoured patterns being geometrical, diamond-shaped medallions, cone shapes, eight-pointed stars; border of three to four stripes; sober colours, blue, brown, yellow, black; Ghiordiz knot; coarse weave.

Balance Wheel   Like the foliot (q.v.) an early form of controller for a clock with a verge escapement; usually a horizontal single-spoked wheel oscillating above a vertical verge.

Ball-and-claw Foot   This termination of a leg in furniture probably derives from the Chinese dragon's claw grasping a ball. First found in English furniture early in the eighteenth century. Sometimes the claw is that of an eagle.

Ball Foot   This ball-shaped termination of a leg in furniture was used in the seventeenth century mainly.

Balloon-back Chair   Victorian, evolving on late Regency, usually straight-legged, swelling curved back nipped-in at waist level; mostly made in sets and in all materials, including papier mâché, metal even.

Baluster   A small pillar, usually of pear- or vase-shape, which may be in a series to support the railing of a balustrade, or in sets as for the legs of a table.

Baluster Stem Pear-shaped decoration on stemmed wooden, pewter, silver or glass vessel or candlestick. On drinking glass stems, the baluster, often inverted, was used in many combinations, with the knop (q.v.), throughout the eighteenth century.

'Bamboo' (1) Furniture. As made in the Chinese style from the middle of the eighteenth century, often with the legs turned to resemble bamboo. (2) Pottery. Stoneware made by Wedgwood that, in colour, had some resemblance to bamboo.

Banding Strip inlay contrasting in colour with background.

Banister-back Chair Chair-back of slender balusters.

Banjo Barometer Barometer case so shaped.

Banjo Clock Wall clock, the casing of banjo shape, invented *c*. 1800 by the American, Simon Willard.

Bantam-work A form of japanning that dates from the seventeenth century; the design incised; the name derives from the Dutch trading settlement in the East Indies through which so much of Oriental lacquer passed on its way to Europe. According to Stalker & Parker (q.v.) Bantam-work was almost obsolete by 1688 (the date of their *Treatise on Japanning*); but they were wrong and the best such work extant dates from the middle of the eighteenth century. (Also called 'Coromandel'.)

Barbeau French for cornflower and applied to the cornflower pattern frequently employed at Sèvres, Chantilly and elsewhere.

Barbotine Potter's technique in slip decoration, the clay being squeezed through the fingers and worked in detail after being applied.

Barometer An instrument for measuring atmospheric pressure and, with luck, forecasting weather. The principle of the mercury barometer was discovered, reputedly by accident, by

Torricelli *c*. 1643. By the 1660's experiments were being conducted in England to produce an instrument that would displace the inaccurate weather-glasses of the time. These experiments led to several types of barometer: the Cistern or Torricellian barometer in which the bottom of the vertical glass tube is immersed in a cup or cistern of mercury, the height of mercury in the tube being read against a graduated scale near the top of the instrument; the Inclined or Diagonal or Yard-arm barometer, like the cistern type but with the addition of a horizontal tube inclining at an angle greater than a right angle from the top of the vertical tube; the Syphon barometer, which differs from the cistern type in that the bottom of the tube does not terminate in a cup of mercury but curves upwards again to form an inverted syphon.

These three basic types were made from the end of the seventeenth century, the syphon principle being adopted for the wheel barometer as early as 1670 (though the wheel type, with hands like a clock, did not come into general use until well into the eighteenth century). Many of the great English clock-makers made barometers—Tompion, Quare, Jones, etc., and cases of walnut and mahogany were often elaborately decorated, ormolu-mounted, gilded, japanned, carved. (The compact aneroid barometer was invented about 1844.)

'Baronial' Furniture *See* **Abbotsford.**

Baroque Useful but overworked term to describe a style in art that is spirited, dynamic, dramatic, bold, sumptuous, ornate. The baroque originated in Italy and precedes the rococo (q.v.); it was based on the classical style and its evolution consisted in the throwing off of classical models—it was a bid for freedom. The heyday of the baroque was from the end of the sixteenth century to the early part of the eighteenth century. In England the influence ranges from Carolean silver to the furniture designs of William Kent.

Basalts Black stoneware perfected by Wedgwood and very popular for decorative vases, figures, medallions, plaques.

This ware was an improvement on the black stoneware made by Elers (q.v.) and was later copied by several makers.

Bas Relief   Modelled decoration in low relief.

Basse Taille Enamel   *See* **Enamel.**

Bateman   Family of London silversmiths. Hester (1709–94) was active 1760–90 and is esteemed for being an early exponent of an austere, plain style, simple and functional. She had two sons who worked in the family business, Peter and Jonathan; then there was Ann, wife of Jonathan, and Ann's son William who was a silversmith of repute in early Victorian times.

Bat Printing   Form of transfer printing used in the decoration of ceramics. In England the process dates from the 1770's. The name derives from the fact that the impression was transferred from a copper plate to the work by means of a 'bat' of gelatine.

Battam Ware (maker's name)   Of red or buff clay, imitating ancient Greek pieces; mid-nineteenth century. Thomas Battam may have evolved the formula for Parian ware when working for Copeland.

Battersea Enamel   Painted enamel, the product of a factory set up about 1753 by Stephen Theodore Janssen at York House, Battersea, London. Janssen went bankrupt and the concern was offered for sale in 1756. Objects decorated in this manufacture had a copper base which was coated with tin enamel on which decorative detail was painted or, more usually, transfer-printed. Robert Hancock worked at this factory. Snuff-boxes, watch cases, wine labels, are typical. Battersea are the most esteemed of English painted enamels.

Baxter Prints   Nineteenth-century colour prints from wooden blocks for each oil colour, the process being the invention of George Baxter (1804–67).

18

Baxter, Thomas China painter active in the early years of the nineteenth century at Worcester particularly, and at Swansea. He excelled at flowers, feathers and shells, landscapes.

Bayonet The bayonet as a broad-bladed dagger with wooden handle for sticking into a musket barrel can be very old— *c.* 1580, but at the end of the seventeenth century a Frenchman invented the modern bayonet which fitted into a tubular socket and not into the barrel.

Bayreuth A faience factory was founded in this Bavarian town in the early years of the eighteenth century and continued in being until well into the nineteenth century (cream-coloured wares in the English manner were made from the 1780's). The usual mark includes the name 'Bayreuth' which is often abbreviated.

Baywood Term sometimes applied to Honduras mahogany to distinguish it from other varieties. *See* **Mahogany.**

Bead Small, *plain* quarter-round or half-round moulding used as decoration on furniture; often called *beading*, particularly when in a sequence.

Bead Moulding Moulding like a string of beads. 'Bead and Reel' moulding is the term when the 'beads' are alternately rounded and oblong.

Bead Work Purses, tea cosies, cushion and stool covers, banner screens, bell-pulls, mantel drapes, lamp shades, various items of female wearing apparel (including garters), caskets, baskets—these items and many more are to be found ornamented with beads. Few examples earlier than the eighteenth century survive.

Beaker Tall cup without handles, the sides tapering outwards from the base.

Beaufait (Buffet)   A term used in the eighteenth century for a recess for the storage and display of glass and ceramics. It is defined in the *Cabinet Dictionary* (1803) as a piece of furniture with covered doors in the lower portion and tiers of shelves above. But associated with food throughout the ages.

Beauvais   A centre of tapestry-weaving in France. A factory was founded there, reputedly with state aid, about 1665, and throughout the remainder of the seventeenth century and most of the eighteenth century produced tapestries that were the finest being made in France. Important figures associated with Beauvais were Béhagle, Oudry, Boucher. Tapestry covers for furniture are a feature of the eighteenth and nineteenth century.

Beech   A timber of light brown colour, tough but easily worked. It takes stain well and was much used for stained, painted and gilded furniture. (First used about the middle of the seventeenth century.)

Beleek   The porcelain factory founded in 1857 at Beleek, Co. Fermanagh, Ireland, to exploit the possibilities of the local china clay and felspar. The felspar was of considerable purity and permitted a very thin and extremely translucent ware which, covered with a thick glaze, has a unique pearly sheen. The factory traded as D. McBirney & Co. The mark incorporates an Irish round tower, the harp and greyhound and three-leaved shamrock.

Bellarmine   A pottery jug with narrow neck and large belly and a bearded mask on the neck. Made principally in Germany and Holland but also at Fulham (q.v.) in the second half of the seventeenth century.

Bellows   Engines 'to make wind' are of considerable antiquity but the collector will be fortunate to find a pair of hand bellows earlier than the eighteenth century. The form has changed but little: matching shaped boards, a metal nozzle, extending leather sides—this was the basic form in the early seventeenth century. Carved, inlaid, japanned, embroidered, much skill was spent on the decoration of hand bellows in the seventeenth and eighteenth centuries. Standing bellows were more business-like machines enclosed in a frame and worked by means of a lever or a wheel.

Beneman, Jean Guillaume German-born French cabinet-maker active from 1785 to the end of the century. Commodes were a speciality. Employed by the Crown, he made a lot of furniture for Marie Antoinette.

Bentley, Thomas (1730–80) Merchant and connoisseur who in 1769 entered into partnership with Josiah Wedgwood, a partnership which lasted till Bentley's death. *See* **Wedgwood.**

Bentwood Steam-heating process (an Austrian invention) by which wood could be bent or curved, introduced into England about 1850 and popular at once, especially for chairs. Birch wood used a lot, with cane backs and seats; sometimes glossy black, sometimes stained to imitate mahogany.

Bérain, Jean French designer active in the second half of the seventeenth century. He must have been one of the first specialists in interior decoration, but was much more than that: he piloted public taste from the Baroque to the Rococo and his influence on the design of ceramics, furniture, tapestries, clothes and the fine arts in general was to go on making itself felt long after his death and in most of the countries of Europe.

Bergama Rugs After Pergamus, whence parchment also came. Sturdy, squarish rugs, dark blue and white on red grounds, long pile, coarse weave (fifty to sixty-five Ghiordiz knots to the square inch); red end webs of Turcoman type, and one to four border stripes geometrically patterned.

Bergère (French) A type of armchair first made in France *circa* 1725; it has a well-rounded back, comfortable padded arms and upholstered sides, sometimes wings as well. In

England the word 'Berger' is often used to denote this kind of chair; but in fact there was a considerable revival in Victorian times when the *bergère* was made with higher back and shorter legs than hitherto.

Berlin Porcelain A Berlin factory was founded in 1752 by one Wilhelm Kaspar Wegely who had the aid of Johann Benckgraff from Vienna and the approval of Frederick the Great. Hard-paste porcelain was made, mostly in the manner of Meissen. The factory closed in 1757. The mark is the letter 'w'.

In 1761 another factory was established, this time by Johann Ernst Gotzkowsky; it was acquired in 1763 by Frederick and became known as the *Königliche Porzellanmanufaktur*, by which name it was known until the First World War when the

Berlin china marks

style changed to *Staatliche Porzellanmanufaktur*. The letter 'G' is the earliest mark (1761–3), then a sceptre until about 1830, after which the letters 'KPM' in conjunction with an orb or a Prussian eagle were used.

Beshir Rugs Turcoman rugs in blue, yellow, red, brown, white; one- to three-stripe border; coarse weave, but these rugs are extremely durable.

Bezel A slope, a sloping face. The groove, flange, lip or ring that holds the glass of a watch or clock, or the stone of a jewel or ring in its setting.

Bianco Sopra Bianco (Italian=white on white) Originally, white pigment decoration used on a white or bluish-white glaze by early Italian makers of maiolica. A popular decoration at

Bristol and some other delftware centres during the eighteenth century, though the ground colour was more likely to be blue or pale grey.

Bidet 'Raised narrow bath that can be bestridden', invented in France early in the seventeenth century. Lavishly decorated examples were made; some carried humorous inscriptions.

Biedermeier A German style of decoration lasting from the Wars of Liberation (1815) to about 1848. In furniture the distinguishing feature is a preference for curved supports in tables, case-furniture and chairs (this curve extending to the chairback).

Bijouterie Jewellery, trinkets. Also a small display case, with tapered legs and a framed, hinged, glass lid, for displaying small objects usually against a velvet lining.

Billet The thumbpiece of a tankard lid; also a moulding consisting of short cylinders.

Billiard Table Billiards is mentioned as early as 1429 in France as an indoor recreation, and the billiard table as we know it, with top covered with cloth and having raised padded sides, was probably being made in France in the fifteenth century. By the middle of the sixteenth century the game was established in England, but the oldest surviving English billiard table (of oak) dates from the end of the seventeenth century.

'Billies & Charlies' A famous range of fakes—lead figures, medallions, etc.—made by two Londoners at the end of the nineteenth century and so popular with collectors that it is said the fakers are now faking the fakes of William and Charles.

Billingsley, William (1760–1828) Maker and decorator of porcelain, born at Derby and apprenticed there at the Derby factory as china painter, advancing to the position of head decorator by 1790, famed particularly for his flower painting. The first of his ventures in the manufacture of porcelain was at Pinxton, then he went to Mansfield and later to Torksey, Lincolnshire, and then to Worcester (about 1808), finally setting up on his own at Nantgarw in 1813, Swansea in 1814, back to Nantgarw 1817–20, then to Coalport, where he worked for John Rose who obtained his formula. He died in poverty in 1828. Billingsley seems the most attractive of all the English arcanists (those who had to work with him probably thought otherwise); he failed and failed and failed again; but the superb Nantgarw and early Swansea porcelain that remains to us is his monument.

Bilston   Town in south Staffordshire where decorated enamelware was produced during the eighteenth century. Much painted enamelware attributed to Battersea (q.v.) was probably made at Bilston in the second half of the eighteenth century. (Bilston was a considerable pottery centre for most of the nineteenth century.)

Birch   A wood that takes staining well and was much used in the eighteenth and early nineteenth century for painted, japanned and gilt furniture.

Bird Cage Clock   A lantern clock, composed entirely of metal, the case being rectangular with a framing of turned angle pillars, the space between the pillars filled in by front and back plates and side doors.

Bird Call   Whistle, often of pottery, in the form of a bird.

Bird's Eye   A veneer patterned with spots.

Biscuit   Porcelain, stoneware and pottery after the first baking and before the application of glaze.

Bismuth   A metal sometimes added to pewter, which it hardens.

Black Egyptian Basalts (q.v.).

Black-glazed Ware Red earthenware body covered with a lustrous black glaze as made in the eighteenth century by Whieldon and other Staffordshire potters and at Jackfield, Salop. Such wares are sometimes called 'Jackfield' wares.

Black Work Black silk embroidery on linen; Tudor; probably introduced into England from Spain and sometimes called 'Spanish Work'.

Blanc-de-chine *See* **Tê-hua porcelain.**

Blobs Pimples of glass applied in molten state to glassware as decoration. Also known as mascaroons, prunts, seals.

Block Foot Furniture leg ending in a rectangular base.

'Blue and White' Pottery and porcelain painted in cobalt blue under the glaze. This form of decoration probably originated in the Near East and was first applied to porcelain by the Chinese in the fourteenth century.

Blue Dash Chargers Tin-enamelled ware circular dishes with a border of blue dashes round the rim, made from the early seventeenth century to the middle of the eighteenth.

Blunderbuss A short musket of large bore flaring at the muzzle, probably first made in Holland in the 1620's. They were never intended to fire nails and odd bits of old iron, but were charged with powder, a wad, a measured quantity of balls or shot and then another wad; no doubt effective at close range, the main idea was to frighten by means of the broad flash.

Bocage The floral or foliage background to figures or groups so favoured by eighteenth- and early nineteenth-century porcelain-makers.

Boccaro The term derives from the name given by the Portuguese to Mexican red pottery and is applied to several types of reddish stoneware, notably the Chinese wares of Yi-Hsing as imported into Europe in the seventeenth century.

Bog Oak Wood obtained from trees found submerged in peat bogs in Ireland.

Bohemian Glass Glass was made in Bohemia from the Middle Ages. Enamelled glass dates from the latter half of the sixteenth century, superb cut-glass from *c.* 1700; *Zwischengoldglaser* or 'gold sandwich' glass was an eighteenth-century development. In the first half of the nineteenth century a great variety of excellent glass was made, cut and engraved, tinted glasses of many types, spun glass and millefiori, glass painted with transparent enamel colours, cased glass.

Bokhara Rugs Turcoman rugs of which there are several types, notably the *Royal Bokhara* which usually has a red ground with blue and ivory patterns, the *Tekke Bokhara*, on which the distinguishing pattern is large and small octagons in blue or ivory on dark red or brown ground, the *Katchli Bokhara*, with the field divided into four by broad bands, the decorative motifs being Y-shaped and in blue on a dark red or brown ground.

Bolection A moulding projecting above the surface of the framework enclosing a panel.

Bolt and Shutter Maintaining Power The device that keeps the power of a clock running for a few minutes while the clock is being wound.

Bombé (French='blown-out') Term applied to furniture with a swelling outline towards the base.

Bonbonnières Small box, often elaborately shaped, for sweet-meats; of gold, silver, enamelled ware, porcelain.

Bone China Hard porcelain rendered soft, or half soft, by an admixture of bone ash; the standard body in England from the end of the eighteenth century.

Bonheur-du-jour A small fitted writing table on tall slender legs; mid-Georgian.

Bonheur-du-jour (*c.* 1790)

Bookcase The bookcase was not made in England to any extent until there was a reading public that demanded it. By the late seventeenth century bookcases were to be found in college libraries and in the homes of a few book-lovers such as Samuel Pepys. The breakfront, or wing, bookcase was an early Georgian contribution, and later there was a demand for a bookcase with the upper stage glazed. The dwarf bookcase, with two or three tiers of shelves, came in during the Regency period.

27

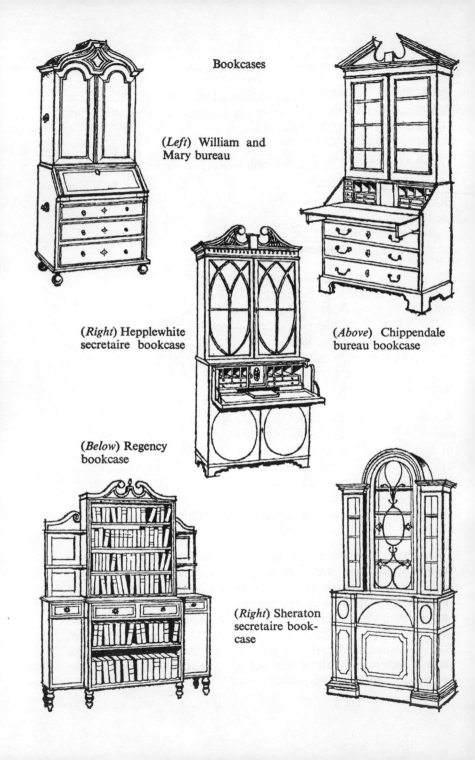

Bookcases

(*Left*) William and
Mary bureau

(*Right*) Hepplewhite
secretaire bookcase

(*Above*) Chippendale
bureau bookcase

(*Below*) Regency
bookcase

(*Right*) Sheraton
secretaire book-
case

Book Rest Portable book rest for the support of large volumes and manuscripts. They were lightly constructed and comprised a squarish frame with horizontal bars pivoting in the uprights, the top bar being attached to an adjustable strut which supported the whole at the required angle. Mahogany usually. Georgian.

Boreman, Zachariah Porcelain painter who worked at Chelsea till its close and then went to Derby and towards the end of the eighteenth century worked in London as an outside decorator. Landscapes were his speciality.

Böttger, Johann Friedrich (1682–1719) Alchemist in the service of Augustus the Strong of Saxony. Unable to produce gold, Böttger was set to work on the porcelain problem and by 1708 he succeeded to the extent of producing white unglazed porcelain, evolving a satisfactory glaze in 1709, in which year he also announced the invention of a very hard red stoneware. The Meissen factory was set up in 1710 to manufacture these wares. *See* **Meissen.**

Boulle Work A process of inlay that derives from the Parisian *ébéniste* André Charles Boulle (1642–1732). This decoration of furniture is a form of marquetry in brass and tortoiseshell or horn, the patterns being cut out of the two materials (fixed together) in one operation. Earliest examples date from about 1680. Ormolu mounts usually go with Boulle furniture. Only a little furniture in the style was made in England, but French workshops produced large quantities of reproductions during the nineteenth century.

Boulton, Matthew Noted eighteenth-century producer of ormolu, silver, Sheffield plate, steel-cut jewellery. Boulton is the only English manufacturer of ormolu who can be seriously compared to the best French makers. He did work to the designs of Robert Adam.

Bourne & Son A firm noted for their stoneware; there were factories at Belper and Denby, Derbyshire; brown salt-glazed wares were a speciality from the beginning (*c.* 1812). The firm is still in existence.

Boutet, Nicolas Noel Eighteenth-century French gun-maker, director of the Royal arms factory at Versailles, whose weapons were superbly ornamental.

Bow The usual date to which the foundation of the Bow porcelain factory is assigned is 1744 and the co-founders are named as Thomas Frye and Edward Heylin, but no porcelain is known to survive from this early period. From 1749 porcelain with bone-ash in the body was produced, often decorated in relief and showing Oriental influences. The early paste is soft, thick, heavy; the products of Bow are much less fine than those of Chelsea; but many figures are lively and their very lack of sophistication finds favour with collectors today. The first use of transfer-printed decoration is often attributed to Bow, but examples are rare. From 1760 onwards a decline set in, there is a greyness about the paste, decoration got out of hand and figures lack the liveliness that is an attribute of Bow at its best.

Bow china marks

Marks are many and confusing: the arrow, the dagger, the anchor, the bow and arrow, the anchor and dagger, the arrow so stylized as to comprise only a circle, a line and a point, the large 'B', the large 'A', many others including workmen's marks (the 'T' and 'T.F.' may be the initials of the founder, Thomas Frye).

It is said that William Duesbury took over the Bow factory in 1776, closed it down and removed the moulds to Derby.

Bow Front   Convex or swell front.

Boxwood   A hard wood of light yellow colour, with close, compact grain and fine, uniform texture; used in marquetry and inlay.

Bracket Clock   A portable clock, a mantel clock. Some such clocks were made with their own matching brackets but survivals are rare.

Bracket Cornice   Cornice supported by brackets.

Bradwell Wood   Probable site in Staffordshire of the Elers' (q.v.) pottery factory where they made their red ware from *c*. 1693 to *c*. 1700.

Branch   Seventeenth- and eighteenth-century term for a chandelier.

Branch Veneer   Veneer cut from the small branches of a tree.

Bras de Lumière   French term for wall-light.

Brass   Alloy of copper with tin, zinc or other base metal.

Brasses   Handles, handle-plates and escutcheons on furniture.

Breakfast Table   A small table with hinged flap extensions supported on brackets; mid-Georgian onwards.

Breakfront   The front line of furniture as broken by projections and/or recesses.

Bristol Glass   Glass was made at Bristol in the late seventeenth century, and one manufacturer, Jacob Little (died 1752), is associated with opaque white glass. The famous 'enamel glass', made at other centres but never so superbly as at Bristol, is dense white, like porcelain, painted with enamels in imitation of china painting. 'Bristol-Blue', now a generic term for any dark blue translucent glass, should strictly be applied to the intense deep blue translucent glass, not necessarily made at Bristol, containing Saxon smalt, produced 1761–90.

Bristol Porcelain (1) *Soft-paste*. The factory (originally a glass-house) founded about 1749 by Benjamin Lund and William Miller. Soaprock was used in the paste. Few examples survive, mostly service-ware, small items like sauce-boats. The marks 'Bristoll' and 'Bristoll 1750' are known. The factory transferred to Worcester in 1752 and wares which cannot be assigned with certainty to one or the other manufacture are designated 'Bristol/Worcester'. The term 'Lund's Bristol' is often used; so is 'Lowdin's Bristol' (William Lowdin was the original owner of the glass-house).

(2) *Hard-paste*. The Plymouth factory of William Cookworthy was transferred to Bristol in 1770. Cookworthy withdrew from the venture in 1773 and it was carried on by Richard Champion until closure in 1782, after which Cookworthy's patent passed to New Hall.

Champion looked to Meissen and Sèvres for his inspiration. Some figures were made, but tableware was the staple product. A wide range of porcelains were manufactured, ranging from lavish made-to-order services to 'cottage Bristol' of a humble kind.

Bristoll 1750

Bristol china marks

The cross in various crude shapes is the main mark, sometimes accompanied by a date or a number. The crossed swords of Meissen were used a lot.

Bristol Pottery   Delftware was made at Bristol from the mid-seventeenth century, first at Brislington and then at Temple Back and Redcliffe and other factories, until the late eighteenth century, from which period and for most of the nineteenth century various types of earthenware were made. The delftware is scarce and difficult to identify; the earthenware is similar to the general Staffordshire wares.

Britannia Metal   An alloy, consisting of 90 per cent tin and 10 per cent antimony, which has a white silvery appearance, invented in the mid-eighteenth century. A cheaper alloy containing 94 per cent tin and 5 per cent antimony has a small addition of copper, which gives it a slightly yellow colour.

Britannia Standard   Adopted for silver in 1697 when, to stop silversmiths melting down the coinage, the standard of purity was raised to 11 oz. 10 dwt. pure silver to each pound troy. The old standard was resumed in 1720, but the Britannia or Higher standard was left optional.

Brocade   Originally a textile fabric with the design worked in gold or silver thread; later, silks so decorated were called brocades. In the seventeenth and eighteenth centuries some furniture was upholstered with brocade covers.

Broken Front   *See* **Breakfront.**

Broken Pediment   A pediment broken by means of omitting the apex, a favoured device with cabinet-makers in the eighteenth century.

Bronze   An alloy of copper and tin in varying proportions but averaging nine parts of copper to one of tin. The ease with which it can be cast and worked have ensured its popularity since Neolithic times.

Broussa Rugs   Silk rugs from or near city of Broussa; Turkish designs, brilliantly coloured and with metallic threads. Ghiordiz knot, 500–600 to square inch, make for fineness and a pile that does not break open when bent backwards. Nor do these rugs curl. Silk fringes.

Brown Bess Musket A long-arm with short wooden stock, precursor of the modern infantry weapon, weight about 10 lb., length of barrel 46 in., equipped with the bridle lock and capable of firing 6 shots a minute but inaccurate beyond 80 yards. This musket was the British Army's principal firearm in the eighteenth century; the name possibly derives from the fact that the barrel was browned by pickling to reduce glare and rusting.

Brussels Carpets Carpets woven as velvet, the looped thread cut to form a pile, but in wool and other coarse materials. This was the type of carpet made at Wilton and Kidderminster (qq.v.).

Buen Retiro Porcelain factory transferred from Capo-di-Monte (q.v.), when Charles became King of Spain in 1759, to the grounds of the royal palace of Buen Retiro, near Madrid. Soft porcelain of good quality was made until the factory closed in 1808. The mark is the fleur-de-lys in various forms.

Buhl *See* **Boulle.**

Bun Foot Flattened version of the ball foot (q.v.); dates from about 1660.

Bureau A French term that appears in England in the late seventeenth century, but it has not been clearly distinguished from other terms such as secretary, *scrutoire* and *escritoire* used for writing desks or cabinets. By 1803 Sheraton could say (in his *Cabinet Dictionary*) that the term was 'applied to common desks with drawers under them'. In combination the word is used for *Bureau-Bookcase, Bureau-Cabinet, Bureau-Dressing-table, Bureau-Table, Bureau-Writing-table, Tallboy-Bureau. A Bureau-plat* is not used of an English piece of furniture but refers to a writing-table with a flat top and drawers beneath as made in France from the beginning of the eighteenth century.

Burmese Glass (*also* **Queen's Burmese**)   Smooth but unpolished semi-opaque ware shading pink to yellow.

Burrs   Knotted wood taken from the outside of the trunk— or the stump—of a tree, which shows a mottled figure, valued for veneering.

Butterfly Table   A table in which the supports for the drop-tops are not the legs but hinged pieces of wood shaped like a butterfly's wing.

Bustelli, Franz Anton (1723–63)   Master modeller at the Nymphenburg porcelain factory from 1754 to 1763 and esteemed as the greatest artist working in porcelain in the eighteenth century. *The* master of the rococo style, he drew his strongest inspiration from the theatre, and figures deriving from the Italian comedy are his masterpieces.

Butler's Tray   A standing tray, often of the X-shaped folding type, 'a sideboard for the butler' made for most of the eighteenth century. A gallery round the top is quite common and some are oval in shape.

Cabaret Set   Porcelain tea set, including a tray, for one or two persons.

Cabinet   A case for the storage of papers and valuables which probably originated in Italy and had found its way to France by the early sixteenth century; made in a variety of forms and sometimes mounted upon a stand.

Cabinet-maker   The cabinet-maker came into his own in the 1660's and by the last quarter of the century the term was in common use. A separate society of cabinet-makers had been formed by the middle of the eighteenth century.

Cabochon A precious stone which is polished but not cut or shaped into a regular figure.

Cabriole A 'leap like that of a goat', a form of chair or table leg which appeared in England in the early eighteenth century;

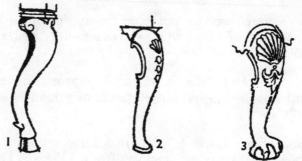

Cabriole. 1, Early, *c.* 1700. 2, Queen Anne. 3, Early Georgian

like a long slow S, the outward curve of the knee sometimes ornamented.

Cadogan Teapot Peach-shaped teapot of Chinese inspiration which filled through a hole in the base. Made first at Rockingham, Yorkshire, in the 1780's.

Caffaggiolo From about 1506 maiolica was produced at or near the Castle of Caffaggiolo, near Florence, under the patronage of a branch of the Medici family.

Calamander Wood Hard, fine-grained wood, light brown with black mottling and stripes, from the East Indies, used for veneer and bandings in Regency furniture particularly.

Calendar Clock Clock that gives the date as well as the time.

Callot Figures Dwarf figures, frequently grotesque, as made at several porcelain factories during the eighteenth century, particularly at Meissen and Vienna. The name derives from Jacques Callot (1593–1635), French artist and engraver.

Cambrian *See* **Swansea.**

Cameo Back One undoubted Victorian contribution to the English chair: open oval back and cabriole legs: from 1840.

Cameo Glass Glassware carved with relief decoration through one or more layers of contrasting colours.

Canapé The French term for a sofa.

Candelabrum A standing branched support for more than one candle. What are now called candelabra were in early times called candlesticks and chandeliers, apparently without distinction; it was not till the nineteenth century that the word candelabra came into use.

Candle Box Box, of oak usually, or some metal such as brass, pewter or even silver, for storing candles. Examples will be found rectangular or cylindrical and will probably date from the eighteenth century.

Candle Stand A portable stand for supporting a light such as a candelabrum. Often in pairs, and as this fashion seems to have come from France the French nomenclature is often used—*Guéridon* or *Torchère* (qq.v.).

Candlestick A support for a candle, at first by means of a pricket or spike, then, from the fifteenth century, by means of a nozzle. In silver examples the wide platform (to catch the grease) tends to disappear by the middle of the seventeenth century; the removable nozzle dates from *circa* 1760. The fluted column, the baluster ornament, were the staples until the classical revival came in in the 1760's (urn-shaped sockets, etc.).

Cane (1) A pliant material made from rattans (a class of palms), introduced into England early in Charles II's reign by the East India Company. When first used the mesh was large but was reduced by the end of the seventeenth century. In 1803, Shenstone mentions a revival of caning for seat furniture. (2) The rods of opaque or coloured glass used in twist-stem glasses and *latticino* glass-making technique generally are called canes.

Canopy A covering, a projection, usually intended for ornament rather than utility. Canopies were often built-in to medieval furniture; but they were also a suspended fabric.

Canteen A small wooden case divided into compartments for carrying bottles. *Also:* a cutlery case for the traveller.

Canterbury Music rack of several vertical divisions, with drawer(s) or shelf beneath, of rosewood, walnut, mahogany; the earliest (late-Georgian) are simple but they grow more and more elaborate with brass or ormolu banding and some are bobbin-turned; much esteemed today for holding periodicals and newspapers. *Also:* supper tray with partitions for cutlery and plate.

Canton One of the most important ports in China and connected by rivers and waterways with the great porcelain-making centre of Ching-tê-Chên; it was therefore only natural that decorating workshops should be established at Canton to take advantage of the export trade to the West. Canton enamelware dates from about 1725. Most of the 'Oriental Lowestoft' was decorated here and the industry flourished well into the nineteenth century.

Capital The head (or top) of a column or pilaster.

Capo-di-Monte A factory for making porcelain set up in 1743 at Capo-di-Monte, near Naples, by Charles, King of Naples. Soft-paste porcelain of excellent quality was made; figures are superb—and very rare. In 1759, when Charles b ecame King of Spain, the factory was removed to Buen Retiro, near Madrid. Early in the nineteenth century the Doccia factory acquired a large number of the Capo-di-Monte moulds and made considerable use of them; but as these Doccia reproductions are hard-paste porcelain their detection should not be difficult. The mark is the fleur-de-lys, also to be used at Buen Retiro (q.v.).

Capstan Table *See* **Rent Table.**

Caquetoire (French) Sixteenth-century chair, with ar ms and tall back.

Carcase The main structure of a piece of fur niture on which veneer is applied.

Cardinal's Hat Broad-brimmed pewtcr dish.

Card-cut (1) Silver. Designs cut in thin sheet-metal and applicd to the body, an ornament introduced in Charles II's reign and fully developed in the first quarter of the eighteenth century. (2) Furniture. Flat ornament applied to or carved on the piece (favoured during the middle years of the eighteenth century).

Card-table A table designed for card playing appears in rare instances towards the end of the seventeenth century, being developed in the early eighteenth century. It had a folding top covered with cloth or velvet and frequently had sinkings for counters and candlesticks.

Carlin, Martin Eighteenth-century *maître ébéniste* who was patronized by Marie Antoinette.

Carlton House Table D-shaped writing-table, the back semi-circular, the straight front containing drawers, the top built up at the back with further drawers and sometimes surmounted by a gallery. Late Georgian and Regency; of mahogany or satinwood.

Carpenter Carpenters made most of the domestic furniture in England until 1632 when a committee of the Court of Aldermen gave joiners the exclusive rights to furniture making, a monopoly that carpenters, especially those outside London, disputed for many long years.

Carpets Said to have been introduced into England by Eleanor of Castile, wife of Edward I. Until the mid-eighteenth century the term 'carpet' was applied to coverings for furniture as well as for the floor. There are two basic methods of carpet-weaving. In tapestry (or smooth-faced) carpets, a loom is used. For pile carpets, rows of knots are tied on the warp thread of a loom and the ends cut down close to the knots, thus forming a pile. After each row is finished weft threads are run through the knots to secure them. Persia and Asia Minor are and have been the great carpet-producing countries, followed by China, India, Spain and France. In England the main manufacturing centres have been Axminster, Wilton, Kidderminster. Separate entries are accorded the more important types and makes.

Carrara Ware The Wedgwood equivalent of *Parian ware* (q.v.); name derives from the white marble of Tuscany.

Cartouche Originally a roll or case of paper, but also applies to an ornament in the form of a tablet representing a sheet of paper with the ends rolled or curled over.

Carver Chair A name given to a heavy, square type of American chair of turned oak, named after Governor Carver's chair at Pilgrim Hall, Plymouth.

Caryatid A standing figure used to support an entablature.

Cased or Flashed or Overlay Glass Layers of different coloured glass laid over a basis of clear glass to which had been applied a thick opaque-white coating. Oblique cutting revealed geometric or otherwise decorative designs; sometimes engraving and deep cutting was an added embellishment. The Romans possessed such a technique; the Bohemian glass-makers made a great deal of cased glass in the nineteenth century; but it was never better done than in England from 1845.

Cassel   German hard-paste porcelain factory active 1766–88.

Cassone   Italian for chest or coffer, an important piece of furniture in the fifteenth and sixteenth centuries and one on which the Italian makers lavished much skill, painted decoration being sometimes superb.

Castel Durante   Famous maiolica centre in Urbino, Italy; the wares produced here in the first half of the sixteenth century are particularly esteemed. Nicola Pellipario, one of the greatest maiolica painters, worked at Castel Durante c. 1712–27.

Castelli   Maiolica producing centre in Abruzzi, Italy, from the sixteenth century.

Caster   A receptacle for sugar and dry condiments such as pepper, having a perforated lid (though sometimes unpierced—for mustard); silver examples may date as early as the late seventeenth century; the use of glass (often with silver lids) became common at the end of the eighteenth century.

Cast Iron as distinct from wrought iron (q.v.), cast iron is hard and brittle and has been 'cast' in a mould.

Castor   Small wheel or roller fitted to a piece of furniture to enable it to be moved without lifting. At first of wood, later of leather in the form of a single roller, then in the mid-eighteenth century a system of leather discs came into use, but gave way, towards the end of the eighteenth century, to brass wheels.

Cat   A three-armed, three-legged stand for warming plates at the fire. Some were made of metal but most are of wood, mahogany particularly, and have elaborately turned arms. Made from the middle of the eighteenth century.

Caudle Cup   Another name for a porringer (q.v.). Caudle was a drink composed of thin gruel and sweetened and spiced wine or ale.

Caughley   This ceramics factory established in the 1750's, produced earthenware until 1772 when Thomas Turner, who had been at Worcester, married the proprietor's daughter and instituted the manufacture of porcelain that at first followed the Worcester style. John Rose of Coalport purchased the Caughley factory in 1799 and kept it in being till 1814, when he transferred the business to Coalport.

There were thus two periods at Caughley. In the first blue and white wares predominated; noteworthy were the 'Willow' and 'Broseley Blue Dragon' patterns which originated here (perhaps the work of apprentice engraver Thomas Minton). In the second period nearly all the porcelain produced was sent in the biscuit state to be glazed and decorated at Coalport.

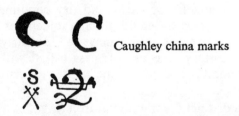

SALOPIAN.

Caughley china marks

The usual mark is the letter 'c', which frequently looks like the Worcester crescent; the letter 's' and the word 'SALOPIAN' are quite common; the marks of several factories were copied.

Cauldron   A kettle, but used for all manner of cooking since earliest times. The cauldron is probably the oldest cooking vessel of all.

Causeuse (French)   A small sofa; a love-seat.

Cedar   Soft, fragrant wood used from the middle of the eighteenth century for the lining of drawers, chests, etc.

Celadon   Chinese porcelain or porcellaneous stoneware with pale bluish or greyish green glaze. Dates from the Sung period and is thought to be the result of porcelain makers attempting to simulate jade. In the eighteenth century the classic Sung wares were copied a great deal.

Cellaret   A term that came into use in the middle of the eighteenth century to indicate a case, with partitions, for bottles; usually on legs; found in many shapes.

Cell Glazing or Cell-mosaic   A variation on the cloisonné enamel technique (*see* **Enamel**) in that the *cloisons* or cells are filled with pieces of glass or stone that have been cut to fit. The French term is *verroterie cloisonné*.

Celour   A canopy for a bed; sometimes used as an alternative term for a tester (q.v.).

Censer   Covered metal bowl for burning incense.

Centre-piece   Silver table piece, often of pierced work, with central basket and several branches; an epergne.

Ceramic   From the Greek *keramos*, pottery, potters' earth. Ceramics is the generic term that covers all forms of pottery and porcelain.

Chaffers, Richard (1731–65)   Potter of Liverpool who made blue and white earthenware and porcelain from Cornish soapstone.

Chaffers, William   Author of the standard work *Marks and Monograms on Pottery and Porcelain*.

Chafing Dish   A portable metal dish, with handles, for heating food.

Chair-table   Chair with back which swings over to form a table. Examples survive from the sixteenth century.

Chaise Longue (French)   A couch or day-bed with upholstered back.

Chalice   Wine cup used at mass; it has a shallow circular bowl and a tall stem.

Chamber Horse   Chair-like contrivance on which to do physical exercises; latter half of the eighteenth century.

Chamberlain, Robert   A decorator at the Worcester porcelain factory who, in 1783, set up his own business, first as a decorator and then as a manufacturer. This venture so prospered that in 1840 Chamberlain & Co. took over the old company (*see* **Worcester**). 'Chamberlain's Worcester' is a typical mark; sometimes just 'Chamberlain's'.

Chambers, Sir William (1726–96)   Architect and furniture designer; author of *Designs of Chinese Buildings and Furniture* (1757); architect of Somerset House.

Chamfer   The canted surface that remains after an angle-edge has been bevelled off.

Chamfron or Chanfron   Head armour worn by horses from the fourteenth to the sixteenth century; an iron spike normally projected from the chamfron.

Champion, Richard (1743–91)   Porcelain-maker who joined with Cookworthy *c.* 1770 in the hard-paste venture at Plymouth (q.v.) and Bristol (q.v.) which he took over when Cookworthy pulled out. But the difficulties were too great and in 1781

Champion sold the hard-paste patent to the company that founded the New Hall factory (q.v.).

Champlevé Enamel *See* **Enamel.**

Chandelier This term, of considerable antiquity, has been applied to a number of lighting fittings but is now confined to lights hanging from the ceiling. The early 'candlebeams' remained in use until ousted by metal chandeliers made chiefly in the Low Countries. Brass chandeliers with S-shaped branches were made in Holland and England in the late seventeenth century and for much of the eighteenth century. With the introduction of cut glass, the use of glass for chandeliers became an important English industry from the early Georgian period until the early nineteenth century.

Chantilly French porcelain factory founded about 1725 under the auspices of Louis-Henri de Bourbon, Prince de Condé, who doted on Arita (q.v.) porcelain and desired that a similar ware be produced in France. Soft-paste porcelain was made, the glaze until the middle of the century being opaque owing

Chantilly china marks

to the incorporation of tin oxide, a practice particular to this factory. Decoration was in the Kakiemon style at first; later, Meissen was the model. The mark is a hunting horn. The factory closed in 1800.

Chapter Ring The brass, sometimes silver, ring set in a clock dial on which the hours and minutes are engraved.

Charger A large plate or dish.

Chatelaine (French = mistress of a *château*) In medieval times a long waist chain with pendant clasp from which hung purse, keys, etc. Victorian ladies dispensed with the waist chain and favoured, hooked into their waist-bands, an ornamental metal plate from which hung several short chains with swivel end-clips for carrying scissors, pencil, keys, scent bottle, penknife, needlecase.

Chelsea The Chelsea porcelain factory was in existence by 1745; silversmiths of French descent seem to have been prominent in the founding of the works; Nicholas Sprimont, who was to become owner, may have been connected with the factory from the start. It is usual to speak of four periods at Chelsea: Triangle 1745–50; Raised Anchor 1750–4; Red Anchor 1754–8; Gold Anchor 1758–70. At first the body was glassy, the celebrated 'moons', or spots of greater translucency, persist until the late 50's when bone-ash was introduced into

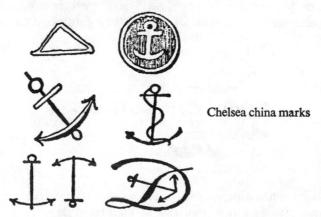

Chelsea china marks

the paste. Oriental influences are strong in the early wares, but by 1750 Meissen tends to be the model and by 1758 Sèvres provides the inspiration.

It is generally agreed that the finest porcelain made in England during the eighteenth century was made at Chelsea.

Figures are particularly esteemed. Many of the best pieces bear no mark. A figure with a fine mark under the base is probably a forgery as it was customary to mark figures inconspicuously low down on the back.

Chelsea-Derby In 1770 the Chelsea works was sold to William Duesbury and John Heath of Derby and the term 'Chelsea-Derby' is applied to those wares thought to have been made at Chelsea after the Derby take-over. The Derby styles soon got the upper hand and many authorities now think that Chelsea quickly became little more than a studio for the decoration of porcelain made at Derby. The Chelsea works closed in 1784.

Chequer (or Checker) Pattern ornament of square sections of light and dark wood—like a chess board.

Cherry Wood of close compact grain and reddish colour, used for inlay, also for making small pieces of furniture.

Chestnut There are two varieties of this tree, the 'horse' and the 'Spanish' chestnut, both having almost white wood; used as a substitute for satinwood in the late eighteenth century.

Cheval A large toilet mirror in a free-standing four-legged frame. These mirrors, also known as *Horse Dressing-glasses*, were first made in the last quarter of the eighteenth century, by which time it was possible to cast single plates of glass six or more feet long, a technical advance that permitted the making of toilet mirrors that would reflect the full height of a person standing close to the glass. In most examples the tall mirror swivels between the uprights on screws, but there is another type in which the mirror, balanced by weights within the uprights, can be moved up and down like a sash window.

Cheveret A small table on slim tapering legs with a removable book-shelf or stand fitted to the top. Incorporated in this stand there may be small drawers (under the shelf proper).

Chiao-tou (Chinese) Three-legged bronze cooking vessel with handles terminating in a dragon's head (Han dynasty).

Chichi Rugs Caucasian rugs with geometric designs in blue, red, ivory, supported with browns and greens; three to five stripe border; Ghiordiz knot and medium weave.

Chien Ware Stoneware of the Sung dynasty made at Chien-an (and later at Chien-yang), Fukein Province. The dark heavy body has an extremely thick black or blue-black glaze streaked with brown. Conical tea-bowls were the principal products, which were prized by the Japanese, who also copied the ware, and gave it the name *temmoku*. Other black-glazed wares from the provinces of Kiangsi, Honan and Chihli are usually termed *Chien* ware.

Chiffonier A tall chest of drawers, quite narrow, the series of drawers designed to contain papers, jewels, or 'chiffons'; not to be confused with the following

Chiffonière A small set of drawers on legs.

Chimney-board A board for blocking the fireplace when not in use, often decorated to match the walls of the room.

Ch'in Dynasty (221–207 B.C.) *See* **Chinese**.

Chinese (Under this heading the main purpose is to give dates —for handy reference. The linking commentary cannot, for reasons of space, be other than a superficial survey of the Chinese achievement. Separate entries are accorded those wares that the collector is likely to encounter.)
Legendary Period (assigned to the third millenium B.C.): hieroglyphic writing, a calendar, silk, pottery, decorated artefacts.
Hsia Dynasty (Legendary—?2200–1766? B.C.): painted pottery, jade, bronze.
Shang-Yin Dynasty (?1766-1122? B.C. or, more likely, ?1600–1000? B.C.): worked in bronze—superb ritual vessels—

ceremonial jade, bone, ivory, stone, clay, tortoiseshell, marble. Money was in use—and a form of writing that is the parent of the present system.

Chou Dynasty (?1122–249 B.C.): great territorial expansion and agricultural development; schools of philosophy and ethics (Confucius ?550–479 B.C.; Taoism a near contemporary school); jade, ceramics, lacquer, mirrors (of polished bronze), inlaid bronzes; iron cutting tools.

Ch'in Dynasty (221–207 B.C.): bureaucracy and censorship; the 'burning of the books'; standardization of the written language and of weights and measures; the Great Wall completed.

Han Dynasty (206 B.C. to A.D. 220): Confucianism becomes orthodox; consolidation at home, conquests abroad; expanding foreign trade and a turning to the West result in textiles and wares reaching the Mediterranean; literature and art flourish; paper invented. The first monumental stone sculpture, glazed pottery, a felspathic stoneware that approaches porcelain, are but some of the achievements identified with Han.

The Three Kingdoms (A.D. 220–80) and *The Six Dynasties* (A.D. 265–581): 'Period of the Warring States'; disunion, wars, foreign invasion; ferment; Buddhism introduced; jewellery, sculpture, painting of a high order; glass imported from the West.

Sui Dynasty (A.D. 581–618): unity again, but the house of Sui soon gives way to the house of T'ang.

T'ang Dynasty (A.D. 618–906), the greatest epoch in China's long history, a golden age in which poetry, the visual and the plastic arts reach new heights; printing invented, paper money introduced. Porcelain invented in the late seventh or early eighth century (a merchant writing in 851 speaks of a clay as fine as glass from which drinking vessels are made and through which the shimmer of water can be seen). T'ang art is vigorous, robust, healthy, full of verve and shows a love of effects; but with the vigour goes restraint, refinement and a disciplined sensibility as regards proportion and the use of colour. Coloured pottery glazes are found in a number of colours—

green, blue, yellow, brown; the glaze frequently has a fine crackle and usually stops short of the foot-ring in an uneven line. Both impressed and incised designs of flowers and birds are typical. Those items of porcelain that have survived, mostly small bowls, are white and translucent true porcelain that must have been fused at a high temperature and contained a considerable proportion of felspar.

The Five Dynasties (A.D. 907–60): wars, internal strife, but the arts flourish, especially painting (landscape, flower subjects).

Sung Dynasty (A.D. 960–1279): the most 'civilized' dynasty of them all thanks to a cultured and cultivated ruling élite. A great period for collecting and cataloguing art of earlier times and this leads to much copying. In painting the landscape of mood is introduced; the weaving of silk tapestries is notable. A rich period for ceramics: Ting ware, celadon, painted stoneware; Sung pottery and porcelain are esteemed for calm unbroken surfaces, classical purity of form, and such techniques as monochrome glazing, painting on slip under the glaze, painting over the glaze, *sgraffito*.

Yüan or Mongol Dynasty (A.D. 1279–1368): foreign rule; the drama and the novel; bamboo painting reaches its peak; Western Europeans arrive in China. The earliest known examples of underglaze blue painting on porcelain date from the end of the Yüan dynasty, as does *shu fu* porcelain.

Ming Dynasty (A.D. 1368–1644): *Ming* means bright. Attempts are made to emulate the great days of T'ang and this results in a Court of unparalleled splendour; there is a love of colour and decoration, rich figured silks and brocades, vigorous sculpture. Porcelain comes into its own, blue-and-white, enamel ware, Fukien wares. The manufacture of porcelain tends to be confined to a single city, Ching-tê-chên, and with abundant china stone and china clay near at hand a huge export trade—chiefly in blue-and-white, celadon, stoneware— is built up, the markets ranging from the Philippines to East Africa. From about 1600 there is the beginning of the export trade to Europe and in 1635 it has been recorded that 129,036 pieces of porcelain were sent to the Dutch possession of

Batavia for shipment to Holland. The reign periods (Hsüan-tê and Ch'êng-hua are most esteemed, followed by Chia-ching and Wan-li):

Hung-wu	1368–98	Hung-chih	1488–1505
Chien-wen	1399–1402	Chêng-tê	1506–21
Yung-lo	1403–24	Chia-ching	1522–66
Hung-hsi	1425	Lung-ch'ing	1567–72
Hsüan-tê	1426–35	Wan-li	1573–1619
Chêng-t'ung	1436–49	T'ai-ch'ang	1620
Ching-t'ai	1450–7	T'ien-ch'i	1621–7
T'ien-shun	1458–64	Ch'ung-chên	1628–43
Ch'êng-hua	1465–87		

Ch'ing or Manchu Dynasty (A.D. 1644–1912): *Ch'ing* means pure, clear. At first there is considerable territorial expansion: Tibet, Nepal, Korea, Mongolia, Manchuria, Turkestan, are all part of the empire. At the same time it is an antiquarian age, scholars devote incredible energy to the compilation of lengthy encyclopaedias and works of learning, there is much looking back, collecting, copying. In painting, the influence of the West is considerable (shading and perspective); in literature, the novel is notable. During the K'ang-hsi period European interest in China and Chinese art reaches its peak ('Chinoiserie'); and under this emperor there is a great revival of ceramics (which had declined at the end of the Ming era) with the rebuilding of the imperial factories at Ching-tê-chên *c.* 1680. For many the most admired wares are those small monochrome pieces that recapture the pure forms of Sung; but there are new colours, turquoise-blue, *sang-de-boeuf* (ox-blood), many others; and, most familiar of all, the much-admired underglazed blue and enamelled wares, the popular blue-and-white 'ginger jars', *famille verte*, *famille noire*, and, later (from the 1720's), *famille rose* (made for export only). The European market becomes more and more demanding; everything is copied, faience, Venetian glass, Delft pottery, Limoges enamels, not to mention the wares of former dynasties; and, of course, armorial china, European motifs, religious

(Christian) decoration. But under three reigns (K'ang-hsi, Yung-chêng, Ch'ien-lung—i.e. from 1662 to 1795) standards remain high, craftsmanship superb; not till the end of the eighteenth century does a decline set in, and by then Europe could supply her own needs from her own factories. The reign periods:

Shun-chih	1644–61	Tao-kuang	1821–50
K'ang-hsi	1662–1722	Hsien-fêng	1851–61
Yung-chêng	1723–35	T'ung-chih	1862–73
Ch'ien-lung	1736–95	Kuang-hsü	1874–1908
Chia-ch'ing	1796–1820	Hsüan-t'ung	1909–12

Ching-tê-chên Porcelain centre in the district of Fou-liang, Kiangsi Province, China. This ancient pottery source came under the patronage of the first Ming emperor, Hung-wu (1368–98) and went on to become the greatest ceramics-making centre the world has known.

Chinoiserie The term means both a vogue for things Chinese and a European-made work of art in the Chinese manner (or what the artist thought was the Chinese manner). The vogue in Europe began quite early in the seventeenth century; the pseudo-Chinese furniture of Chippendale, the 'willow pattern' decoration of Minton and Spode, these are *chinoiseries*.

Chip-carving Faceted surface ornament; rough carving executed on oak and other early furniture by means of chisel and gouge.

Chippendale, Thomas (1718–79) English cabinet-maker and designer whose reputation stands higher than that of any other. He was born at Otley, Yorkshire, the son of a carpenter. It is thought he may have been apprenticed to a London cabinet-maker, but there is no definite evidence of this; what is known is that he married in London in 1748 and soon after that he had rented the premises in St Martin's Lane that he was to retain for the rest of his life. He worked with two partners, first James Rannie and then Thomas Haig. The business was con-

The Chippendale chair

tinued after his death by his eldest son, another Thomas (1749–1822), in partnership with Haig.

While some furniture of superb quality has been identified as from Chippendale's workshops, his great reputation is due to his book of designs, *The Gentleman and Cabinet-maker's Director*. This folio volume was first issued in 1754, reprinted in 1755, and a third enlarged edition was issued in parts between 1759 and 1762. The *Director* was by far the most ambitious work of its kind published up to that date. Practically every type of domestic furniture of the mid-eighteenth century was illustrated. The first edition contained more than 150 plates; the third edition had some 200. Almost all the designs are in the Gothic, Chinese and Modern (rococo) fashions. Just how many of the designs were drawn by Chippendale is a matter for dispute, but the plates are signed by him and in the preface he took the credit for the entire work. It cannot be too often pointed out that 'Chippendale furniture' means furniture corresponding in style to the designs illustrated in the *Director*.

Chocolate Pot   Like the coffee pot but usually a little smaller, and the lid may have an aperture in it to allow a stirring stick to be inserted.

Chou Dynasty (?1122–249 B.C.)   *See* **Chinese.**

Chüeh (Chinese)   Ancient bronze vessel for heating and storing wine, the shape like that of an inverted helmet; has three (sometimes four) pointed feet and a side-handle.

Chün ware   Stoneware of the Sung dynasty that comes close to porcelain; made at Chün Chou, Northern Honan Province. There are several types of ware. The most esteemed has a light grey body and a downward-flowing glaze (which has an irregular lower edge) that is to be found in various shades of grey, blue, violet and red. A lavender glaze with purple mottling is another variety. And a distinct variety has a coarse yellowish or dark body but with a similar glaze to the finer wares.

Clapboard Pine timber imported in board form from the Baltic countries for use in panelling.

Clavichord A small rectangular musical instrument, with strings and a keyboard, that dates from the thirteenth century. The mechanism comprises strips of metal, the tangents, which are attached to the ends of the keys. When a key is depressed the appropriate tangent rises and strikes the string, causing it to vibrate. English clavichords are so rare that the collector can forget about them; but as the instrument continued to be made on the Continent till the beginning of the nineteenth century there is still some scope in that direction.

Claw-and-ball Foot *See* **Ball-and-claw.**

Clay, Henry Inventor of 'Clay's Ware', the first *papier mâché* (q.v.).

Clignancourt Paris hard-paste porcelain factory producing during the last quarter of the eighteenth century.

Clobbered Decoration Overpainting existing decoration on ceramics is termed 'clobbering'.

Clocks The mechanical clock was invented during the last quarter of the thirteenth century, the earliest form probably being the Turret clock designed to be fitted to a church tower or other building. (The clock from Wells Cathedral was made *c.* 1390.) The first spring-driven clock was made about the middle of the fifteenth century. The earliest clocks were of wrought iron, with the use of brass coming in, on the Continent, in the sixteenth century, and in England, at the beginning of the seventeenth century. Few domestic clocks were made in England before the seventeenth century. The first individual English type of weight-driven clock, the lantern clock, had a frame, dial and side doors of brass or iron and was surmounted by a bell; several specimens, made by the famous Fromanteels (q.v.) and dating back to the 1620's, are still in existence, and the lantern clock continued to be made till the beginning of the nineteenth century. The long-case or 'grandfather' clock came in the 1660's, with the pendulum (q.v.). The earliest were thirty-hour movements, but quite soon came the eight-day clock and then those designed to run for a month, three months, six months and (rarely) a year. The spring-driven mantel clock came into favour at about the same time as the long-case clock but few early specimens have survived as they were poor time-keepers and much more liable to damage. Many of these early mantel clocks were intended for the bedroom and contained repeating mechanism; they were an 'extra' in the house, often not much more than trinkets; until the middle of the eighteenth century most had the inaccurate verge escapement because of its one virtue—a clock so fitted could be taken from room to room and set down without elaborate levelling. But from about 1740 the mantel clock stayed on the mantel. There would almost certainly be a mirror behind it, and because of this the backplate lent itself to decoration. The anchor escapement became standard. The number of early mantel clocks with *original* verge escapements must be very few; most were converted to the anchor escapement but some have been reconverted to the verge.

The great age of English clock-making was from 1660 to 1750; the outstanding makers were the Fromanteels, East, Jones, the Knibbs, Tompion, Quare and Graham (qq.v.). The woods used for cases: at first, to *c.* 1685, veneered oak; then from *c.* 1670 to 1770, walnut; from 1760, mahogany. Dials: from 1660 to 1673, 8 to $8\frac{1}{2}$ in. square; from 1673 to 1695, 10 in. square; from 1685 to 1712, 12 in. square; from 1705, rectangular, of greater depth than width. Until about 1710 the hood slides upwards to be removed; from about 1700 it slides forward. The top is likely to have a gable pediment *c.* 1660–75, a flat pediment (carved) *c.* 1665–1730, and to be arched from *c.* 1720.

Cloisonné Enamel *See* **Enamel.**

Close Stool or Close Chair Portable jakes, usually in box form, sometimes on short legs; the term dates from the end of the fifteenth century; the close stool gave way to the Night Table (q.v.) in the first half of the eighteenth century.

Clowes, William Staffordshire potter who made black stoneware (basalts) and pottery generally, and was a member of the company that founded the New Hall (q.v.) hard-paste porcelain factory. Active *c.* 1785 to *c.* 1812.

Club Foot Plain type of foot on furniture, being found with the cabriole or straight leg throughout the eighteenth century.

Coalport This porcelain factory founded about 1796 by John Rose who had been with Thomas Turner at Caughley. In 1799 Rose bought out his former employer and in 1814 transferred the Caughley concern to Coalport. Then in 1820 Rose acquired what was left of the Nantgarw enterprise and so secured Billingsley's recipes and moulds. John Rose died in 1841; his nephew, William Rose, continued the business till 1862, since when it has been in various hands.

The earliest Coalport cannot be distinguished from Caughley with any certainty. Generally speaking the paste is excellent and with a good glaze but there is a lack of aesthetic quality in form and decoration, save in the case of the more famous imitations. Sèvres, Meissen, Chelsea, were all imitated extensively, complete with marks. From *c.* 1840 elaborate dinner and dessert services were a feature, lavishly gilded.

Coalport china marks

Marks include 'CD', CBD', 'Coalport' in long-hand, 'John Rose & Co.' Note that the words 'Coalport' and 'Colebrookdale' are synonymous.

Coaster Small wagon for use on the dining-table. Sometimes fitted with wheels, but examples are more likely to have a polished wooden base (which were originally covered with baize). They are to be found in various shapes and often with compartments to hold glasses, bottles. Also called *sliders*.

Cobalt Blue Glass Opaque hard blue ware; very heavy; can be mistaken for china.

Cobb, John (?–1778) Cabinet-maker who, in partnership with William Vile (q.v.), was in business a few doors away from Chippendale (q.v.) in St Martin's Lane. Marquetry commodes were a speciality. He did work for George III.

Cobirons Articles of chimney furniture, a form of andiron but for the kitchen, usually having hooks on the standards and a shaped top to take a cup or pot.

Cock-beading Small moulding used round the edge of drawers; introduced about 1730.

Coffee-pot Dates from the second half of the seventeenth century; it was always tall (early examples are straight-sided, conical) and has never lost height like the tea-pot.

Coffer The distinction is sometimes made that a coffer as opposed to a chest should be covered with leather and laced with metal bands. A *Coffer* is also a sunken panel.

Coffer Bach A box for a bible.

Coin Term sometimes used in the eighteenth century for a corner cupboard; derives from the French *encoignure*.

Coin Glass *See* **Knop.**

Colebrookdale *See* **Coalport.**

Collier A form of necklet popular in the nineteenth century.

58

The coffee pot. 1, 1808. 2, 1731. 3, 1715. 4, 1783

Collier Revolver Invented by the Bostonian Elisha Collier *c*. 1814 and developed in England by Evans from 1819 onwards. This flintlock is considered the true ancestor of revolvers.

Colt Revolver A percussion revolving pistol as made by the American, Samuel Colt. Most esteemed are his early 'Paterson' models, made at Paterson, New Jersey, 1836–42. Colt went bankrupt but returned to firearms in 1847 when the Mexican War brought him a contract for 1,000 revolvers and thus began the famous enterprise at Hartford, Conn., where all Colts were thenceforth made except for those produced at the London factory between 1853 and 1857.

Combed Decoration   Ceramics decoration; a pattern used on the borders of plates and dishes in which curved parallel lines are stroked in towards the centre of the piece as if by a comb.

Commode   A French term, applied to a low case of drawers, described as a new word in 1708. The commode was adopted in England in the reign of George II and illustrated in the *Director* (1754 and 1762); japanned, inlaid and painted commodes were a feature of late Georgian furniture.

Cone Beaker   Early northern drinking glass (without a foot) which probably displaced the drinking horn.

Confidante   A sofa with a seat added at each end (and often set at an angle to the sofa). The idea seems to have been that the added seats could be detached and used as easy chairs; but in some examples the extra seats are not removable. The fashion probably came from France in the 1770's. Not many were made.

Console   A bracket (usually of scroll shape in profile).

Console Table   A side-table partly supported by and usually fixed to a wall; the front supports are usually two legs of bracket shape.

Cookworthy, William (1705–80)   Arcanist, Quaker; born at Kingsbridge, Devon, and became an apothecary, but with an interest in the manufacture of porcelain from at least 1745. In the 1750's he discovered china clay and china stone on the estate of Lord Camelford in Cornwall and in 1768 founded his hard-paste porcelain factory at Plymouth (q.v.), later transferring to Bristol (q.v.).

Copeland *See* **Spode.**

Copenhagen A soft-paste porcelain factory founded at Copenhagen about 1759 with the aid of the French modeller Louis Fournier who had been at Chantilly and Vincennes. This venture came to an end in 1765.

The hard-paste factory which is still in existence was established in 1774 and became the Royal Copenhagen Porcelain Manufactory in 1779. The famous Flora Danica service, comprising about 1,600 pieces, was produced here 1789–1802. Copenhagen porcelain is noteworthy for its high glaze, subdued colours with pearly tints, superb modelling of figures, especially animals. Three horizontal wavy lines are the famous mark.

Coquillage (French=shell-fish) A shell-like ornament to be found on furniture of the mid-eighteenth century; favoured as a central ornament of a seat rail.

Corbel A projection jutting from a wall or a piece of furniture and intended to take a hanging weight.

Cordial Glass A small, delicate glass from which to drink cordial, i.e. liqueurs, first made in the 1670's. (It was customary to serve tea and cordials together throughout the eighteenth century.) Like miniature wine glasses, though the flute form became popular in the second half of the eighteenth century.

Corner Chair *See* **Roundabout Chair.**

Corner Cupboard Cupboards made for the corner of a room were known in the seventeenth century and became quite common during the William and Mary period. They were popular throughout the first half of the eighteenth century, both hanging and standing, lacquered often, sometimes in burr walnut veneer. They went out of fashion in the second half of the eighteenth century but, of course, continued to be made in country districts.

Cornice   The uppermost member of an entablature in classical architecture, and applied to furniture in the same way.

Coromandel   (1) *Wood.* Ebony imported from the Coromandel coast of India and used for banding; favoured during the Regency period; blackish with light stripes. (2) *Lacquer.* Incised Oriental lacquer popular in England from the second half of the seventeenth century; 'Bantam-work' (q.v.) is the more usual term.

Corona   Term for a hanging light, a metal hoop, used in churches and grand homes in medieval times.

Couch   The term was in use in the sixteenth century but it is difficult to be sure if the meaning had any other than that of day-bed; it may have been more grand. In the eighteenth century men seemed to prefer the term day-bed, ladies the term couch. During the Regency period the classical couch came into favour—by way of France.

Counter   Table or chest, the top of which was designed with spaces and symbols as aids in the counting of money. The counter dates from the Middle Ages and was popular till the end of the sixteenth century.

Court Cupboard   A term used in the Elizabethan and Jacobean periods for a side-board for the display of plate and for vessels in use during meals.

Crackle   (1) In porcelain, the crazing of the glaze intentionally for decorative purposes. (2) In pottery, the crazing that may take place, often long after manufacture, as a result of the unequal contraction of glaze and body. (3) In glass, an effect produced by the sudden cooling of the surface of glass when still not completely blown.

Cream Jug The silver cream jug was introduced at the beginning of the eighteenth century, the helmet shape being popular; by the middle of the century three feet are common, the lip is elongated and pointed, the handle has broken curves; the jug grows more and more slender, almost vase-like, and the feet disappear or become diminutive; then by the turn of the century the cream jug has a full, low body.

Creamware Cream-coloured earthenware, supposedly first made by Thomas Astbury, but brought to perfection by Josiah Wedgwood who manufactured it on a large scale from the middle of the eighteenth century and by 1765 was exporting quantities of the ware to Europe where, more than any other single factor, it brought the manufacture of faience to an end. Also called 'Queen's ware'.

Credence (Italian *credenza*=cupboard) A small table by the altar side on which the bread and wine were set before consecration. The term has also been applied to a side table for the arranging of food and drinks to be served at table. English examples of the domestic credence are extremely rare.

Creepers (chimney furniture) Small andirons standing between large andirons (q.v.).

Cresset An iron lamp like a basket in which a fuel was burnt; usually fixed to a rod.

Cresting The carved decoration at the head of a piece of furniture, such as the top rail of a chair, or the ornament at the head of a mirror.

Crewel-work Form of embroidery in fine worsteds popular throughout the seventeenth century for bed hangings.

Crich or Crouch Ware Salt-glazed stoneware which may have been made at Crich in Derbyshire.

Cristallo Venetian, from early sixteenth century, the superb, clear, ductile glass that was Venice's greatest contribution to glass-making.

Croft (maker's name) A small writing-desk-cum-filing-cabinet made at the end of the eighteenth century—a dwarf piece of furniture.

Cross-banding Banding of veneer in which the grain of the band runs across that of the ground. Popular throughout the eighteenth century.

Crown Wheel (horological) The escape wheel in a verge escapement. *See* **Escapement.**

Crunden, John Furniture designer, published *The Joyner and Cabinet-maker's Darling* in 1765.

Crystallo Ceramie Process of encasing a small object such as a cameo in a solid block of clear flint glass; the best made by the inventor of the process, Apsley Pellatt, between 1819 and 1835.

Cumming, Alexander (1732–1814) Scottish-born clock-maker who made many fine timepieces including the remarkable astronomical clock commissioned by George III and now in Buckingham Palace.

Cupboard A cupboard was an open structure with shelves in the Middle Ages and what we would today call a cupboard was known as an almery (q.v.) or aumbry. The use of cupboard in the modern sense did not become general until the beginning of the seventeenth century.

Curfew A metal cover for placing over embers in the fireplace; perhaps used for safety but more probably to keep the embers alive during the night. The earliest known example dates from the first half of the seventeenth century. Rare.

Curule A seat shaped like a camp-stool, used by Roman magistrates. In the *Cabinet Dictionary* (1803) a chair of different form, with semi-circular back and elongated seat, is illustrated as a curule chair.

Cutts, John Porcelain and pottery painter who was manager of the Pinxton factory (q.v.) and did work for the Wedgwoods.

Cyma Recta Moulding comprising two curves, the upper concave.

Cyma Reversa Moulding comprising two curves, the lower concave.

Cypress Fine-grained wood of reddish colour and great durability.

Damascening Metal decorated by inlays of gold and/or silver wire, the design being undercut into the surface to be decorated and the precious metals hammered into the grooves. This form of decoration is of great antiquity and is often found on weapons.

Daniel Family of Staffordshire potters, the most notable being Henry Daniel (1765–1841) who founded the firm of H. & R. Daniel in the early nineteenth century and made stone china and creamware and some porcelain.

Darly, Mathias A man of many talents and trades including those of designer and engraver. His publications include *A New Book of Chinese, Gothic and Modern Chairs* (1751), *A New Book of Chinese Designs* (1754) and *The Compleat Architect* (1770). He engraved most of the plates for the first edition of Chippendale's *Director*.

Davenport (1) A small writing desk, intended for the use of ladies, comprising a chest of drawers with a sloping top. Date from about 1800; the earliest examples are high and square and sometimes have brass galleries. The desk portion can extend on a train. Often the drawers pull out at the side and the other side will be fitted with dummy knobs.

(2) The ceramics factory founded at Longport by John Davenport in 1793; pottery only made at first, but good quality porcelain, and 'stone china' for a larger market, produced from the early years of the nineteenth century. The printed

Davenport china marks

name 'Davenport', often with an anchor, is the usual mark; the crown appears after 1830 (the firm made lavish services for royalty). The factory closed in 1882.

Day-bed Dates from Jacobean times; was popular during reign of William and Mary when it usually had caned seat and back (the back rest often adjustable).

Deal Term given to two varieties of the Scots pine, yellow and red deal, used for the carcase of veneered furniture; the yellow was in use until the middle of the eighteenth century, the red after that. Deal is also a piece (or a number of pieces) of sawn pine or fir wood measuring more than 7 in. wide and not more than 3 in. thick.

Decanter 'Crystal' decanters, then called bottles, were being made in 1677, and the word appears in 1701 and is defined in 1715 as a bottle made of clear flint glass for the holding of wine, etc., to be poured into a drinking glass. The ordinary form between 1675 and 1750 has a narrow neck and globular body. Shortly before 1720 a form with sloping shoulders and shorter neck was introduced. The finest date from 1790–1820.

Delft (England) Tin-enamelled earthenware made from the mid-sixteenth century, first at Norwich and then at Lambeth and Southwark in London, and then, from the mid-seventeenth to the mid-eighteenth century, at Bristol, Wincanton, Liverpool. Though the first makers were probably Dutch or Flemish, the name delftware was not given to the ware until well into the seventeenth century, by which time Delft in Holland was a famous pottery centre. (*See next entry*.)

Delft (Holland) Tin-enamelled earthenware made at Delft from before 1600 but notably from the mid-seventeenth century to the mid-eighteenth. The ware was an attempt to copy Chinese and Japanese porcelains at first and decoration was in the Oriental manner; but later European subjects were used and the baroque and rococo styles are to be observed. Marks divide into two classes, those based on the signs of the breweries in Delft that housed the first great potteries such as De Blompot (the Flower Pot) and De Vergulde Boot (the Golden Boot), and marks which represent the initials of the potter, 'A.K.', 'H.B.', 'M.P.' A clearly marked piece, especially if it has the name 'Delft', is probably modern.

Derby The origins of porcelain-making at Derby are obscure; some authorities suggest the year 1745. By 1756 the enterprise was under the direction of William Duesbury and John Heath. In 1770 the Chelsea factory was purchased; in 1776 (or 1778) Bow was the victim, being closed down. About 1780 Heath went bankrupt and Duesbury continued as sole owner till his death in 1786 whereon his son, another William, took over and ran the factory until his death in 1796. But the latter had thoughtfully taken a partner in 1795, and this partner, Michael Kean, married his widow and continued the business for some years. William Duesbury III was briefly at the helm, for a time with a partner, William Sheffield, but then the concern passed into the hands of Robert Bloor and stayed there until Bloor's mind failed him about 1827. James Thomason took over the management, later jointly with Thomas Clarke, and kept things going till the factory closed down in 1848. The extant Royal Crown Derby Porcelain Company was established in 1877.

Early Derby shows the influence of Meissen via Chelsea and then Meissen direct. About 1770 bone-ash was introduced into the paste. Figures were a speciality, at first based on Meissen originals, then on Sèvres (the notable biscuit figures); many have 'patches' under the base, due to the fact that the figures were placed on pads of clay (three, sometimes four) in the kiln. Painted decoration of a high order was characteristic right up till the end of the eighteenth century. Japan patterns were favoured, and revived successfully by the Crown Derby Company. It is usual to speak of a deterioration after the turn of the century. Note that strictly speaking 'crown Derby' are wares produced by the Crown Derby Porcelain Company.

Derby china marks

Marks are rare on early Derby, but 'D' and 'Derby' have been observed, a 'D' with an anchor running across it (Chelsea-Derby?); the crown seems to date from the late 1770's, with various devices beneath it—an anchor, a 'D', a cross with dots, the monogram 'DK' (Ducsbury & Kean), a 'B' (Bloor). The Meissen mark is often found.

Derbyshire Chair   *See* **Yorkshire Chair.**

Deruta   Pottery centre on the Tiber in Umbria, Italy, famous for its wares since medieval times. During the first half of the sixteenth century maiolica produced here was of excellent quality. Deruta lustre wares are notable.

Desk   The feature of a desk is that it has a sloping front to support a book or writing materials, and until the first half of the seventeenth century the desk (pure and simple, as it were) was the only piece of furniture made specifically for writing. As distinct from the desks in university and cathedral libraries, the domestic desk as a personal possession was a small portable box with sloping lid until the introduction of bureaux in the last quarter of the seventeenth century.

Dessert Glass   Glasses for dessert were made from the beginning of the eighteenth century. Those with deep bowls were intended for such sweets as ice-cream and custards, whereas those with shallow saucer-like bowls were for such sweetmeats as could be picked up in the fingers. The scalloped rim was popular.

Diaper   (1) A fabric woven in a small pattern consisting of lines crossing diamond-wise enclosing a space filled with simple ornament. (2) This pattern used as decoration.

Disbrowe, Nicholas (?1612–72)   One of the earliest American furniture makers; born in Essex; emigrated in 1630's; worked and died at Hartford, Conn.

Dished Corner   Depression near corner of table-top to hold counters (or a candlestick).

Dish-top   Table top with raised rim.

Divan   Low, cushioned seat of Eastern origin; a backless sofa deriving from Eastern styles and intended to be placed against a wall.

Doccia   Porcelain factory near Florence, Italy, founded about 1735; made soft-paste porcelain at first but a harder paste was introduced towards the end of the eighteenth century. The wares of other factories were much copied at Doccia, particularly those of Capo-di-Monte (q.v.). The mark often includes the name 'Ginori', which family were associated with the factory from the beginning.

Dole Cupboard Term applied to a food cupboard as was to be found in churches in the sixteenth and seventeenth centuries for storing food to be doled out to the poor.

Dolls *Wax*. First made in England at end of sixteenth century, the base usually of wood or metal; in the early nineteenth century *papier mâché*, and later, composition bases were used. The best wax dolls have a flesh-tinted colour, glass eyes inset, and hair (human) of head, eyelashes and eyebrows inserted hair by hair. *China*. Few pre-nineteenth-century examples survive. Most nineteenth-century china dolls were made in France and Germany. Two outstanding makers, both French, were Jumeau and Bru. *Wooden*. Made from very early times; some that have survived look like skittles. Good hand-carving indicates quality. Ball-and-socket joints are a quite recent innovation. *General*. The first 'walking' doll, the first 'talking' doll, the first with eyes that opened and closed, all made in the 1820's. Weighted eyes introduced in the 1870's. Dolls were formerly called 'babies' but not till the nineteenth century were actual baby dolls made.

Dolls' Houses The earliest English examples that survive date from the first half of the eighteenth century.

Dolphin Foot The head of a dolphin as terminal for legs of furniture was used in the eighteenth century, and the head and body were used for decorative effect in late Georgian and Regency times.

Donaldson, John Edinburgh-born (1737) porcelain painter, a noted miniaturist whose work on Worcester vases is highly esteemed. He also did some work at Chelsea.

Don Pottery   A factory at Swinton, Yorkshire, founded about 1790 and continuing, mainly under the direction of the Green family, till the 1890's. Creamware of good quality was made, pierced work in the manner of Leeds, also stoneware and china.

Doulton   Ceramic wares produced at Vauxhall and then at Lambeth, the driving force behind the business of Doulton & Watts being John Doulton (1793–1872). Typical are relief-decorated stoneware jugs, salt-glazed stonewares, particularly ornamental pieces; but, of course, even more typical are the sanitary products of this well-known firm.

Dovetailing   A cabinet-maker's favoured method of joining two broad, thin pieces of wood together at right-angles by means of bedding the end of the first member (comprising small, cut-out tenons shaped like a dove's spread tail) into prepared cavities in the end grain of the second member. There are two basic types of dovetail, the 'through' dovetail in which the ends of the tenons go through to the far side of the cavities and are thus visible on the outside of the second member, and the 'stop' dovetail in which the tenons stop short a little way from the far edge of the second member and are thus invisible from that side as the cavities are made exactly to fit. The second method was employed on quality work from the end of the seventeenth century, the first method having been usual before then.

Dowel   A headless pin or peg which serves to fasten two pieces of timber together by piercing some distance into the connected members.

Dram-glass   A short drinking glass with, often, the lower half of the bowl solid. Made from the latter half of the seventeenth century—for strong waters. Also called dram-cup, dram-pot, dram-dish, joey, ginette.

Draw Table   The earliest form of extending table. The leaves lie beneath the main top and when pulled out are made to rise and come flush with the main top by means of tapered bearers. From Elizabethan times, and still one of the most reliable of extending table forms.

Dresden   The English name for Meissen (q.v.). Best used for later Meissen, the nineteenth century figures particularly. Throughout the centuries there have been many potteries at or near Dresden, notably Böttger's faience manufactory established at Neustadt in 1708.

Dresser   Originally a board or table on which food was *dressed*; later, (1) a table from which dishes were served, and (2) a provincial side table, usually surmounted by rows of shelves.

Dressing Box   A box for toilet requisites, often with a mirror in the lid.

Dressing Table   Dressing tables are listed as a distinct variety in inventories of the middle of the seventeenth century. In the early Georgian period, tables of knee-hole pedestal type often had a drawer fitted with compartments and a mirror, and by late Georgian times small tables with a hinged box lid were made in quantities.

Drinking Glasses   Two main classes, (1) beer glasses, usually of tumbler shape, and (2) stemmed glasses intended for wine, ale and cordials. The evolution of the English wine glass from the late seventeenth century is extremely complicated, but, simplified, the trend is from capacious bowls and short stems to smaller, slimmer bowls and longer, more sophisticated stems. Decoration on stems from 1680 to 1725 includes the true and inverted baluster, often with enclosed 'tear', and many variations and combinations of the knop. Air-twist stems were an important development of the late 1730's; and opaque-twist stems came into favour in the next decade, followed by colour-twist stems. Cut and faceted stems date from about 1745, hollow diamond patterns being much used till *c*. 1770, then fluted patterns till *c*. 1800, when raised diamond patterns and prismatic cutting came in.

The drinking glass. 1, Ale glass, *c.* 1690. 2, Wine glass, shouldered stem, *c.* 1725. 3, Wine glass, rummer type, *c.* 1710. 4, Baluster wine glass, *c.* 1690. 5, Ale glass, *c.* 1770. 6, Wine glass, *c.* 1775. 7, Wine glass, air twist stem, *c.* 1750. 8, Goblet, 'acorn' baluster stem, *c.* 1710. 9, Ale glass, *c.* 1770

Drop-handle Pear-shaped handle of the late seventeenth century.

Drop-in Seat The removable chair seat dates back to the early eighteenth century.

Drop-leaf Table Table with one or two hinged leaves as extensions.

Dropped Seat Chair seat shaped to fit the body.

Drum Table *See* **Rent Table.**

Dubois, Jacques Eighteenth-century French cabinet-maker noted for his lacquered furniture. His son, Réné, was also a *maitre-ébéniste* and made furniture for Marie Antoinette. The two are often confused (the son used the father's stamp).

Duchesse According to Hepplewhite (his *Guide*, 1788) a duchesse was formed of 'two barjier (*bergère*, q.v.) chairs of proper construction with a stool in the middle'. It is a couch with tub-shaped ends, usually removable, linked by a square stool.

Duesbury, William (?1725–86) An important figure in the evolution of English porcelains. The son of a Longton (Staffordshire) potter, he was, in the early 1750's, running an outside decorator's business in London, and by 1756 he had control of the Derby factory. He purchased the Chelsea concern in 1770, and also took over what was left of Bow.

Duelling Pistols As distinct from ordinary twin or ornamental sets, these lack over-bright or over-heavy ornamentation and have perfect balance so that they will 'come up' accurately when fired according to the strict rules of the duel.

Dumb Waiter A stand with tier of circular trays from a central stem, probably an English invention where it was in use as early as the 1720's. Three trays are normal, though some examples have four, and they grow progressively larger from top to bottom.

Du Paquier, Claude Arcanist and founder of the Vienna Porcelain Factory (q.v.). Porcelain made at Vienna under his directorship (1717–44) is sometimes called 'Du Paquier porcelain'.

Duvivier Family of Belgian porcelain painters who worked in England. William came to England about 1743 and worked at Chelsea; his son, Henri Joseph, born at Tournai, learned the craft at Chelsea and later returned to his birthplace to practise there. Fidèle Duvivier, cousin of Henri Joseph, did work for various English factories—Chelsea, Derby, Worcester, Pinxton, New Hall.

Dwight, John (?–1703) In 1671 John Dwight of Fulham was granted a fourteen-year patent for making stoneware and he seems to have been the first to produce in England a semi-translucent ware that approaches porcelain. A few superb busts and figures survive (a measure of their excellence is that they have been attributed to Grinling Gibbons). Dwight also made red ware, Cologne ware (a grey earthenware imported from Germany for domestic use), and various stonewares decorated in relief. His Fulham factory remained in the family till 1863.

Earthenware The oldest ceramic substance; pottery of baked clay too porous to use in biscuit state and requiring glaze; unvitrified pottery (*see* **Stoneware**). Earthenware is usually classified according to the glazing and decoration that is added to it—e.g. slipware, creamware, delft, faience, maiolica (qq.v.).

East, Edward 'Watch-maker, Citizen and Goldsmith of London.' Born at Southill, Beds., 1602, he was famous first for his watches (watch-maker to Charles I), later for his clocks; the workmanship was always superb.

Easy Chair   The term dates from the late seventeenth century or early eighteenth century as applied to a chair 'adapted for ease or repose'. In Sheraton's *Cabinet Dictionary* (1803) we read of a tub-shaped chair 'stuffed all over and intended for sick persons, being both easy and warm. . . '.

Eaton Hall Chairs   As designed by A. Waterhouse for Eaton Hall in 1867. Circular seat; curved, padded back rails and arms which form a semi-circle; usually of mahogany; luxuriously upholstered; short, turned legs.

Ébéniste   The French term for cabinet-maker, literally meaning one who works in ebony, it came to imply one who worked in veneers.

Ebonise   Staining wood to look like ebony.

Echinus Moulding   Quarter-round moulding.

Écuelle   Continental type of silver porringer and cover, shallower than the English and with two flat, pierced handles. Huguenot silversmiths introduced the écuelle into England.

Egg-and-dart and Egg-and-tongue   Ornamental moulding of alternative egg-shapes and dart or tongue shapes.

Egg-shell Porcelain   Porcelain of extreme thinness as first made in China at the beginning of the fifteenth century (the Yung Lo period) and again under K'ang-hsi, Yung Cheng and Ch'ien Lung (1662–1795). Certain nineteenth-century English factories—especially Minton—produced egg-shell wares.

Egyptian Black   Basalts (q.v.).

Elers, David and John   The Elers brothers, from Holland, are said to have been silversmiths originally, but by 1690 they were active as potters making red stoneware in London. In 1693 they moved to North Staffordshire and continued to make, at Bradwell Wood, the red ware with which their name is associated, until about 1698.

Empire The style and period of the first Empire in France, say 1794–1830. The furniture was based on styles of antiquity, much use being made of wreaths and pateras, urns, winged figures, clawed feet, brasses, mahogany, rosewood.

Enamel Made by fusing a paste of powdered glass on to a base of metal, usually copper, bronze or gold. *The basic technique*: moistened paste is spread over the metal base, the object fired in a kiln and the heat melts the paste which adheres to the metal. The art of enamelling is of considerable antiquity and probably had its origins in Greece and/or Etruria between the sixth and third centuries B.C. The most important classifications are: (1) *Cloisonné*, in which the design is divided by metal strips, soldered on to the ground, forming small compartments, or *cloisons*, which are filled with enamel; (2) *Champlevé*, in which small compartments are hollowed out of the ground, to keep the enamels separate; (3) *Basse Taille* or *En Plein*, in which the ground is first carved or engraved at a slightly sunken level which is 'topped up' with enamel; (4) *painted enamels*, in which pictures or designs are painted upon an undercoat of white enamel; (5) *plique à jour*, in which translucent enamel is strengthened by internal strips of metal—like stained-glass windows.

Encaustic Burned-in colour.

Encoignure French term for a corner cupboard (q.v.). Popular for the greater part of the eighteenth century.

En Plein Enamel *See* **Enamel.**

Epergne Centre dish for the table, often having branches which support small dishes or baskets for sweetmeats, etc.; of silver usually, or porcelain.

Escapement The means of control over the driving force of a clock or watch; the device that permits the power to 'escape' to the pendulum or balance. The first mechanical escapement was the *Verge*, said to have been quite well known by 1350, in which two pallets alternately trap and release a saw-edged tooth of the crown wheel (the escape wheel). Its worst feature was that it never left the pendulum free, whereas the ideal escapement is that which leaves the pendulum free for the greatest length of time. There were many attempts at improvement but not until 1671 did William Clement invent (or perfect) the *Anchor* escapement, so called because the curved arm and two pallets suggest the head and flukes of an anchor. This was a great step forward. There was less interference with the escape wheel. The wide swing of the verge escapement pendulum, which kept the pendulum short, was replaced by the long, slow-swinging pendulum moving through an arc of as little as four degrees, thus minimizing error and allowing for a beat of one second (and the second hand) and the evolution of the long-case clock. The only fault was the shudder or recoil caused by the jarring that accompanied the engagement of the pallets with the teeth of the escape wheel. Hence the next improvement, the *Dead Beat* escapement, a modification of the anchor escapement, in which the pallets bed 'dead' on to the escape wheel teeth and abolish recoil or jarring, thus making for greater accuracy. Invented by George Graham in 1715 the dead beat escapement is still in use today. It should be noted that clocks were often converted when a marked technical improvement was invented; but there will normally be evidence of the conversion.

Escritoire *See* **Scrutoire.**

Escutcheon (1) A shield-shaped surface on which a coat-of-arms, cypher or other device appears. (2) A metal plate pierced for a key-hole.

Espagnolette (French) Gillot and his pupil, Watteau, made fashionable this decorative motif of the stiff lace collar worn by Spanish women. It developed into a pattern used by furniture designers and is to be found on Régence writing tables and chests of drawers.

Étagère Decorative drawing-room table with one or two graduated tiers above main top, the separating pillars usually ormolu; of satinwood, kingwood, tulipwood, mahogany; legs, usually cabriole, sometimes straight tapered, ormolu-mounted.

Etruria The name Josiah Wedgwood gave to the factory (and village that grew up round it) he opened in 1769. He chose this name because he wished to revive the pottery-making art of the Etruscans.

Étui Small box for the use of ladies; fitted with compartments to contain scissors and other personal objects; of pinchbeck often but also silver, porcelain, etc.

Ewer Usually with basin or dish. The most common form is the swelling vase shape with small mouth but largish lip and handle curving quite tightly to reach a higher point than the top of the vessel; the helmet shape is frequently encountered.

Ewery Cupboard The ewer and basin (see above) stood on this low cupboard which contained toilet accessories.

Faenza One of the most important Italian maiolica centres from 1450. The French term *faience* (q.v.) probably derives from the Italian town.

Faience Pale red earthenware covered with a tin glaze. The term dates from the beginning of the seventeenth century (though the ware was made at least 100 years earlier) and is thought to derive rather from the Italian town of Faenza than from the French Fayence. Faience was made in several European countries during the sixteenth, seventeenth and eighteenth centuries but outstandingly in France from *c.* 1700 to 1780; the main centres were Nevers, Lyons, Marseilles,

Montpellier, Aprey, Rouen, Sceaux. Tablewares were the main products. Until the middle of the eighteenth century the principal colours were green, yellow, orange, blue; but after 1750 crimson, pink and vermilion came into use. *Faience anglais* was an attempt to copy English cream-coloured wares (Faience fine); *Faience Japonnée* was decorated in the Oriental manner; *Faience parlante* and *Faience populaire* were decorated with songs, sayings, proverbs, etc.; *Faience porcelaine* was an attempt to imitate real porcelain by means of rich enamel overglaze decoration.

Famille Jaune Chinese porcelain dating from the K'ang Hsi period in which a yellow ground was used for the polychrome enamel decoration. Examples are rare.

Famille Noire Chinese porcelain dating from the K'ang Hsi period in which a black ground (washed with transparent green enamel) was used for the polychrome enamel decoration. Examples are rare—especially of the greatly esteemed large vases with floral designs.

Famille Rose Chinese porcelain dating from the K'ang Hsi period, but associated mainly with the Yung Chêng and Ch'ien Lung periods, and so-called because of the use of a new colour (a European innovation), *rose*, an opaque pink enamel. The Chinese called this colour *yang-ts'ai* (foreign colours) and *famille rose* wares were made for the export market only. Much of the decoration was done in the studios of Canton. At its best the painting is extremely delicate; European subjects are quite common.

Famille Verte Chinese porcelain of the K'ang Hsi period so-called because it exhibits the predominant use of a brilliant green enamel. The *verte* palette is a development of the Ming *wu-ts'ai* (five-colour) decoration, but the Ming underglaze blue gives way to overglaze blue enamel. *Famille verte* wares (at their best) are mainly responsible for the great esteem which attaches to the K'ang Hsi period. The paste is fine, the potting

PLATE 1. An Oak Stool of the Elizabethan Period. (*In the Collection of Mary Bellis*)

PLATE 2. Georgian Silver. *Top shelf:* George II and III Cream Jugs, George II Oil and Vinegar Frame; *Centre shelf:* George III Pair of Candlesticks and Salver, George II Pair of Salt Cellars; *Lower shelf:* George III Coffee Pot, Pair of Candlesticks, and Taper Box. (*Photograph by permission of Hicklenton & Phillips, Cheapside, London*)

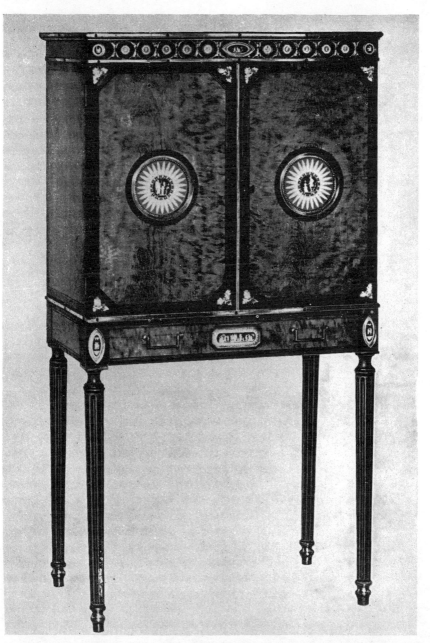

PLATE 3. Adam satinwood Cabinet, ormolu-mounted and inset with Wedgwood plaques. (*Photograph by permission of J. W. Blanchard, Esq., of Winchester*)

PLATE 4. Examples of First Period Worcester Porcelain. (*Photograph by permission of Trevor Antiques of Brighton*)

PLATE 5. A Pair of early Georgian carved mahogany Stools. (*Photograph by permission of Messrs. M. Harris & Sons of London, W.C.*1)

PLATE 6. (*Right*) A Regency Work Table in faded Rosewood inlaid with brass stringing, *circa* 1810. (*Photograph by permission of E. W. J. Legg, Esq., of Dorchester*)

PLATE 7. (*Below*) A selection of mid-eighteenth century engraved English Drinking Glasses, including (*right*) a scarce Privateer specimen and some typical Jacobite examples. (*Photograph by permission of Cecil Davis Ltd., of London, W.*1)

PLATE 8. (*Above*) Pair of Hepplewhite Armchairs. (*Photograph by permission of Louis Brown, Beaconsfield, Bucks.*) PLATE 9. (*Below*) Dresden Tea-set, with toilet and writing requisites, in original case, *circa* 1790. Intended for coach travelling. (*Photograph by permission of Roger Warner, Esq., Burford, Oxon.*)

PLATE 10. Examples of K'ang Hsi famille verte Porcelain. (*Photograph by permission of W. Waddingham, Esq., London and Harrogate*)

PLATE 11. A
Queen Anne Card
Table in finely
figured Walnut,
circa 1715.
(*Photograph by
permission of
Frank R. Shaftoe,
Harrogate*)

PLATE 12. A mahogany Library Table of *circa* 1760, attributed to Vile and Cobb.
(*Photograph by courtesy of W. Waddingham, Esq., London and Harrogate*)

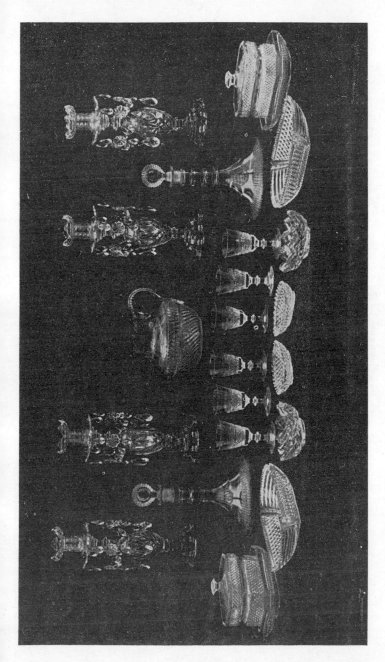

PLATE 13. Antique Glass: this selection includes a set of four Irish Candle Lustres of *circa* 1780, a pair of Ships' Decanters, and a pair of Irish Butter Dishes. (*Photograph by courtesy of John Fileman, Brighton*)

PLATE 14. Eighteenth-century Antiques: carved pine Mantel, "Chinese Chippendale" Elbow Chair, Wine Bucket, and nest of "Quartetto" Tables. (*Photograph by permission of Margery Dean, Wivenhoe, Essex*)

PLATE 15. *Left to right:* Silver Coffee Pots: Queen Anne 1707 by Tho. Parr; George I 1726 by Tho. Mason; George II 1752 by Ayme Videau; George III 1784 by Langlands & Robertson. (*Photograph by permission of William Walter (Antiques) Ltd., London Silver Vaults*)

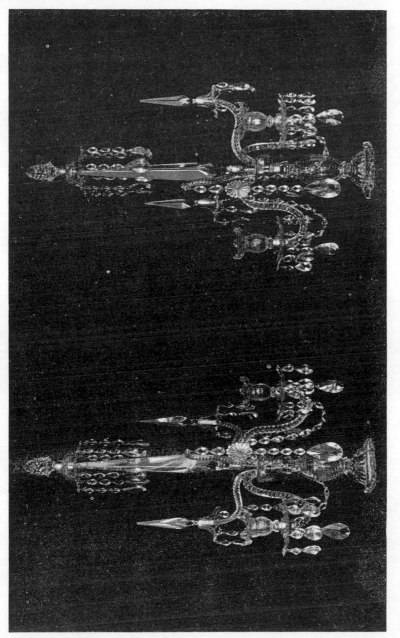

PLATE 16. A pair of Glass Candelabra, 27 inches in height, of *circa* 1790. (*Photograph by permission of John Fileman, Brighton*)

PLATE 17. Dutch silver Salt Cellar of *circa* 1618, made by Adam Van Vianen. (*Photograph by permission of Joseph M. Morpurgo, Amsterdam*)

is of a high order, the decoration, whether vigorous or delicate, is superb.

Fan Back   Windsor chair back, flared like a fan.

Farthingale Chair   Chair without arms, with quite a wide seat and with narrow, high back; so-called because built to accommodate females in farthingales, for whom any other kind of scat was well nigh an impossibility.

Fauteuil   French term for an arm-chair; but when used precisely, an arm-chair whose sides are not, in contradistinction to the *Bergère* (q.v.), upholstered.

Feather Banding   *See* **Herring-bone.**

Fender   The wide hearth made fenders unnecessary till the late seventeenth century, but in the eighteenth century steel fenders, shaped, pierced and engraved, became common. Brass fenders, with bottom plates, came in the late eighteenth century. In the 1820's Birmingham began the manufacture of cast iron fenders which was to put an end to the decorative fender.

Feraghan Rugs   Persian rugs in which the red or dark blue ground is decorated with floral or foliage designs; three-stripe border usually; a coarse weave woven with the Senna knot.

Festoon   A garland of flowers, leaves, fruit, etc., loosely suspended between two points—hence a representation of similar ornaments in carving, stucco, painting.

Finger Vase   Vase consisting of five flower holders arranged as are the fingers of a hand. Made at Delft and other ceramics centres.

Finial   An ornament projecting from a roof or gable; hence applied to a similar ornament heading a canopy or piece of furniture, or the knob in the form of an acorn or even a human figure that tops a vase or cup cover or the end of a spoon.

Fire-back or Fire-plate or Reredo Cast-iron slab placed at the back of a fireplace to protect the wall and to throw the heat forward. Early examples are wide and quite low, usually rectangular in shape; the tombstone shape came in in the late seventeenth century. And it is at about this time that many fire-backs were imported from Holland. Sussex was the traditional place of manufacture in England and some of the best early examples are in Sussex museums, Hastings particularly. The designs were impressed on the bed of sand (in which the plate was moulded) by means of movable wooden stamps.

Fire-dog *See* **Andiron.**

Fire-fork The forerunner of the poker, a lengthy iron two-pronged fork for adjusting burning logs in the fireplace; went out of use when coal came in in the eighteenth century.

Fire-irons Equipment for use at the fireside: fork (when wood was the fuel—see previous entry), tongs, shovel (when coal became the fuel), and brush. Tongs are the most elaborate item in most sets. Examples survive from the seventeenth century.

Fire Pan A tray for holding burning charcoal.

'Fire Polish' The brilliant finish that is imparted to glass by repeated re-heating after it has begun to cool.

Fire Screen Both the pole screen and the cheval screen were made to protect the sitter from the heat of an open fire. *See* **Screen.**

Firing-glass Short, stubby drinking glass so made to withstand rapping on the table when toasts were being drunk.

Flagon Formerly a bottle to hold liquor; later a tall drinking vessel with a handle and usually a lid; forerunner of the tankard.

Flambé French term meaning singed, passed through flame.

Flambé Glazes Glazes found on certain Chinese ceramics, such as vivid reds streaked with blue or purple. In early wares, as of the Sung dynasty, it is probable that these effects were unintended but brought about by uncertain kiln conditions; later, from the eighteenth century, they were brought about intentionally and were very popular during the Ch'ien Lung period.

Flashed Glass *See* **Cased Glass.**

Flaxman, John (1755–1826) Sculptor employed by Wedgwood to design many of the relief decorations for the jasper ware.

Flintlock A type of gunlock which dates from the early seventeenth century. The pan holds priming powder and has a hinged cover from which rises a piece of steel; a flint is held in the jaws of a cock; when discharged the flint strikes the steel and at the same time throws the cover back thus allowing the sparks to shower into the priming. *See* **Snaphaunce.**

Flora Danica *See* **Copenhagen.**

Fluting A decorative motif much used on silver vessels, also on furniture, comprising channels divided by a sharp fillet.

Foliot Early form of mechanical clock controller which went with the verge escapement.

Fontainebleau French hard-paste porcelain factory founded in 1795.

Form The form or bench (the terms are interchangeable) is a seat with supports or legs which has remained essentially the same throughout its history. In early times the form was sometimes a plank resting on trestles.

Frankenthal Porcelain factory founded at Frankenthal near Mannheim, Germany, in 1755 by Paul-Anton Hannong, who had produced porcelain at Strasbourg, with the aid of J. J.

Frankenthal china marks

Ringler of Vienna. The factory purchased by the Elector Palatine in 1762; it closed in 1799.

Fretwork This form of decoration was used a lot by eighteenth century English cabinet-makers, particularly when the Chinese and Gothic tastes were in vogue. Open fretwork, as on galleries of small tables, was usually made from several thicknesses of veneer glued together. Decorative fretwork patterns on a solid ground were used on a variety of furniture—chair legs, for instance.

Frieze Member of an entablature coming between architrave and cornice.

Friggers Improbable and even fantastic objects made of glass —tobacco pipes, walking sticks, bells, ships, riding crops, bellows (flasks), rolling pins—much else. Made at Nailsea particularly, and at Bristol, and to a lesser extent at other glass-making centres.

Frit A calcined mixture of sand and alkalis as used for glass-making and in the manufacture of soft-paste porcelain.

Frog Mug Type of mug made mostly at Sunderland, but also at Leeds, Nottingham and elsewhere, containing a model of a frog.

Fromanteels, The The London branch of this famous family of Dutch clock-makers established itself in England in the

1620's and for almost 100 years practised their craft with distinction.

Frye, Thomas Irish painter turned porcelain manufacturer who in 1744 registered jointly with Edward Heylyn a patent for making porcelain (*unaker* was a specified ingredient) and later in 1749 patented another formula which included calcined bones. In partnership with two London merchants Frye founded the factory at Bow (q.v.), which he managed until his retirement in 1759.

Fu (Chinese) A rectangular bronze container, usually on four feet. Chou dynasty.

Fuddling-cup A number of cups cemented together with openings one to the other; made at Lambeth, Bristol, and other pottery centres in the seventeenth and eighteenth centuries.

Fulda A porcelain factory founded at Fulda, Hesse, Germany, in 1765. The venture was under the auspices of the Prince-Bishop of Fulda, Heinrich von Bibra. The factory was burned down in 1767 but was rebuilt and continued until 1790. A hard paste of excellent quality was made and figures are highly regarded. 'FF' linked to form an 'H' is the usual mark.

Fulham This stoneware factory founded in 1671 by John Dwight (q.v.).

Furnishing Pieces A trade term applied to antiques which, because their price is within the purse of most collectors, can be bought for use in the home. Such a piece would therefore usually be less than perfect and of somewhat doubtful provenance.

Fürstenberg This porcelain factory founded in 1747 at Fürstenberg, Brunswick, Germany, under the auspices of Duke Karl I of Brunswick, but no porcelain was produced until the arrival of Johann Benckgraff (who had been at Vienna) in 1753. Hard-paste porcelain was made from this date, but not very successfully till *c.* 1770. However, during

Fürstenberg china marks

the period 1770–1800 much excellent porcelain, including figures, was manufactured. The letter 'F' is the usual mark.

Fusee A device that equalizes the pull of the mainspring of a clock or watch. The spring would go too fast when fully wound and too slow when almost unwound were it not for the fusee, a pulley to which the strain is transferred and whose conical shape transmits a steady pull to the train. Invented in the fifteenth century and still in use in clocks of quality.

Fustian A coarse cotton cloth used for bed hangings and counterpanes in early times; later the term seems to have applied to a richer material used as the outer cover of upholstery and even for clothing. Norwich was a prominent manufacturing centre of fustian in the fourteenth and fifteenth centuries.

Fustic Wood imported from Central America and the West Indies and used for a time during the eighteenth century as a veneer; but its yellow colour, which presumably commended it at first, was found to be impermanent and the wood was no longer used by the end of the century.

Gadrooning Convex curves in a series used as an ornament carved on the edge of furniture (also as an enrichment of silver). There are two varieties, the upright and the waved.

Gallipot   Small jar, usually with handle, used by apothecaries.

Gardner, Francis   Englishman who founded a porcelain factory in Moscow *c.* 1758.

Garnish   Strictly, a complete set of *pewter* comprising a dozen platters, a dozen bowls and a dozen small plates; but the term is also used to indicate a set of plates and dishes generally.

Garniture de Cheminée   Set of five porcelain vases, two beakers and three with covers. First made in China and copied by European factories in the eighteenth century.

Gate-leg   Term applied to an oval (sometimes round) table with drop leaves and extra legs on hinges at either side which swing out to support the raised leaves. Usually of oak.

Gather   The blob of molten glass that the glass-blower 'gathers' on the end of his blowpipe.

Gesso   A preparation of chalk worked into a paste with parchment size, used as priming before colouring or gilding furniture. In the late seventeenth and early eighteenth centuries the gesso coat on mirrors, side-tables (and more rarely seat furniture) received low relief carving before gilding.

Ghiordes Rugs   Turkish, multi-coloured, often with floral designs, the warp and weft sometimes of silk.

Gibbons, Grinling   (1648–1720)   Sculptor and wood-carver, born in Holland but emigrated to England in reign of Charles II; was employed in the royal palaces of Windsor, Whitehall and Kensington and other great houses. He was noted for his ornate carving—wreaths, swags, pendants, elaborate acanthus leaves, cherubs' heads, animals and other figures, all with extreme delicacy of touch. Some of his best work may be seen in the choir-stalls of St Paul's.

Gilding The extreme malleability of gold permits a thin skin of it to be fixed to a plaster ground. The two chief methods of gilding with gold leaf are (1) Water, and (2) Oil gilding. Water gilding is applied over a ground of size and whiting to which a paste of red clay and parchment size has been added. When dry, the surface is made wet and the gold leaf applied. In oil gilding the piece is painted with gold size, left on for some hours, and the gold leaf applied when still tacky. The surface is then spirit-varnished with size.

Giles, James Eighteenth-century decorator of ceramics. Much Worcester porcelain was painted by Giles in his London workshop.

Gillow, Robert (?–1772) English cabinet-maker, established in Lancaster 1724, transferred to London 1756. His son, Richard, is credited with the invention of the modern telescopic dining-table, *c*. 1800.

Gimmal A finger ring so constructed that it can be divided into two (occasionally three) rings.

Gimmel Twin glass flask (the two bottles blown individually and fused together) with two spouts which usually face in opposite directions; much made at Nailsea, but dates back to the seventeenth century, perhaps earlier.

Giobu Japanese lacquering technique which gives a mottled effect.

Girandole (1) French term for wall-light or elaborate candlestick. In the trade catalogues of the second half of the eighteenth century, elaborate wall-lights, often with a mirror back-plate, are described as girandoles. (2) Ear-ring or pendant comprising a large central stone from which hang small ones.

Glass A brittle lustrous substance made by fusing silica (sand) to which has been added a flux such as soda or potash. The main characteristics of glass are that in its molten state, when it is sticky like honey, it can be easily fashioned, it can be drawn out into threads as thin as a hair, it can be blown like a bubble, and it welds easily and inseparably. It is easy to colour. An Egyptian or Syrian invention, glass-making dates back to at least 2500 B.C.; it was valued at first because it could be made to approximate precious stones; vessels of considerable aesthetic appeal were made as early as 1500 B.C. The blow-pipe was invented during the first century B.C. The Romans made excellent glass in every part of their empire. In the Near East glass of a high artistic standard continued to be made throughout the 'dark ages'; there seems to have been a continuing tradition, too, in areas of northern Europe round the Rhine and the Seine. But the great revival in Europe was to take place at Venice and, to a lesser extent, at Altare, near Genoa. By the thirteenth century the Venetians were supreme, at first with coloured glass, then painted enamel glass, *millefiori*, *aventurine*, 'ice-glass', the superb *cristallo*, *latticino*.

English Glass. Some crude domestic glass was probably made after the Roman withdrawal, but even by the twelfth century most stained window-glass was imported from France. For fine table glass England had to await the arrival of Giacomo Verzelini and his band of Venetian workmen in 1571. After a troubled start he acquired royal patronage when, in 1575, Queen Elizabeth granted him a licence 'to make drinking glasses in the manner of Murano, on the undertaking that he bring up in the said art and knowledge our natural subjects'. Verzelini kept to the bargain and during the twenty years that followed made much fine glass and a good deal of money and won a great deal of respect. But he did not create an industry; this feat was performed by Sir Robert Mansell who held the monopoly from 1618 till the advent of Cromwell. Mansell brought prices down; he welcomed new ideas and processes, the making of mirrors, of wine bottles; he encouraged coal-mining to provide his industry with fuel. After the artist and the business man came the technologist, George Ravenscroft, who first made flint glass, the celebrated 'glass of lead', about 1675. Though it could not be blown as thin as the Venetian *cristallo* it was more durable, its softness lent itself to deep cutting, and it had a greater brilliance and richness. It was a glass that was to allow the English genius its full expression. It enabled England to become an exporter and by the end of the seventeenth century some 100 glass-houses were making lead glass. London, Bristol, Stourbridge, Birmingham, Newcastle upon Tyne, and other centres, were in the glass business. (*See* particularly **Drinking Glasses** for later developments.)

German Glass. In the Middle Ages *Waldglas* was the staple, green, brown, yellow, design evolving from low, Roman shapes to tall, vertical Gothic. The great German glass-making centres were Bohemia, Saxony, Silesia, Potsdam. Painting with enamels dates from the sixteenth century, particularly in Bohemia and Saxony. Like the English, Germanic glass-workers strove to make their own equivalent of the Venetian *cristallo*, and about 1680 a new formula was discovered, in Bohemia, which brought success. Chalk was added to the mix and potash replaced soda; the resultant glass was suited to deep cutting and had a hard brilliance. By the beginning of the eighteenth century engraving of a high artistic standard was being done in Bohemia, Silesia and Potsdam. Opaque-white became popular about this time.

Dutch Glass. As German till the early seventeenth century when many Venetian glass-workers settled in Holland where the Italian styles were to be later influenced by German and English techniques. The great Dutch and Flemish contribution to glass-making was in the excellence of their engraved decoration; whether working with diamond point or wheel their work, at its best, has never been surpassed. Much of it was done on English-made glass; stipple-point engraving was notable in the latter half of the eighteenth century and, indeed, well into the nineteenth century.

French Glass The French, undisputed masters of stained-glass making in the Middle Ages, contributed little to domestic wares. The Italians made *cristallo* at Paris, Rouen, and particularly at Nevers; but the French themselves did not participate and were for centuries content to import enormous quantities of glass from Germany and England. However, it was a

Frenchman, Bernard Perrot, who invented plate glass at the end of the seventeenth century. And in the nineteenth century the French did more than any other race to evolve new forms and revive old ones: *pâte de verre* (glass paste), decoration in relief, the blending of soft colours, the influence of Japanese art.

American Glass. Made from the beginning of the seventeenth century. Glass was manufactured on Manhattan Island from 1645. The bottle was all during the eighteenth century, and is to the American collector what the drinking glass is to his English counterpart. 'Baron' Stiegel, a German who went to America in 1750, probably made the first flint glass in the New World *c.* 1765. He was a financial failure, but his name in 'Stiegel glass' has become generic for early American glass. Pressed glass (q.v.) was an American invention, being first made about 1827, reputedly by Enoch Robinson.

Glastonbury Chair   Chair with X-shaped supports, the upper extensions of which form the arms and link with the back. The term derives from Glastonbury Abbey.

Glaze   A glass-like substance, usually containing lead, applied as a thin skin to the surface of most pottery and porcelain.

Gobelins   Gobelin was the family name of Belgian dyers who migrated to Paris in the fifteenth century, establishing a tannery and later a tapestry manufactory. This and several other Parisian workshops were united in 1667 by Jean Baptiste Colbert, a Minister of Louis XIV, to form a *manufacture royale* under the direction of Charles Le Brun. Le Brun was an excellent artist and personally designed some of the cartoons for the superb tapestries produced. Under Le Brun and other directors (notably Oudry) Gobelins retained its great reputation until the late eighteenth century.

Godet   Obsolete term for a drinking cup or jug.

Going-cart   A 'baby cage' on wheels for teaching a child to walk; made from the Middle Ages and quite common in

England by the seventeenth century where they were popular till the end of the eighteenth century.

Gombron Ware European term for pottery and porcelain from Persia and China in which the walls of bowls and the like were pierced and filled in with a translucent glaze. Gombron was a port on the Persian Gulf from which the wares were shipped to Europe.

Gothic The style of architecture, of which the pointed arch is preponderantly typical, that prevailed from the twelfth to the sixteenth century in Europe and which influence is to be seen in furniture and metalware of that time. There was a Gothic revival in England in the second quarter of the eighteenth

Gothic stool

century (it co-existed rather strangely side by side with Chinoiserie, q.v., and the Rococo, q.v.) and this influence is to be seen at its strongest in some of the furniture designs of Chippendale. There was a second Gothic revival in Victorian times. When the result of the Gothic influence is too awful the word is often spelt with a 'k' on the end.

Gout Stool Foot stool, usually of the X-frame type, for the afflicted, for whom such stools were specifically made in the Georgian period.

Graham, George (?1673–1751)   English horologist who succeeded Tompion as the foremost clock-maker of his day; invented the dead beat escapement (*c.* 1715), the cylinder escapement for watches (*c.* 1725), the mercury pendulum (*c.* 1726).

Grainger, Thomas   Founded early in the nineteenth century a porcelain factory at Worcester which traded as Grainger, Lee & Co. and made porcelains in the style of Chamberlain (q.v.). In 1889 the factory was taken over by the Royal Worcester Co.

Graining   This process of painting a cheap wood to reproduce the grain, colour, texture and figure of a more esteemed and costly wood goes back (in England) at least to Elizabethan times when oak and walnut were thus counterfeited. The practice continues.

Grain-of-rice   Ceramic decoration as found on Gombron ware (q.v.) and practised by Persian and Chinese potters.

Grandfather Clock   Nineteenth-century name for a long-case clock.

Grandmother Clock   A small long-case clock.

Grand Sonnerie Striking   A sequence of clock striking that strikes the quarters *and the hour* at every quarter.

Grate   This item of chimney furniture became necessary when coal came into use, and though few examples exist earlier than the mid-eighteenth century the grate was known at the beginning of the seventeenth. The basket-grate, of iron or steel, was usual till the late eighteenth century when the hob-grate came into favour, at which both types were made till well into the nineteenth century.

Grisaille   Painting in grey to represent objects in relief (e.g. the medallions on painted furniture).

Gubbio Important maiolica centre in Urbino, Italy, being famed in the sixteenth century for lustre wares. Ruby and golden lustres of great brilliance were the specialities.

Guéridon, also Guéridon Table A slender piece of furniture for supporting a light such as a candelabrum. The name is said to have been that of a Moorish galley-slave and early Guéridons were made in the form of a negro figure.

Guilloche Ornament consisting of two or more intersecting curved bands twisting over each other and repeating the same figure in a continued series.

Gumley, John Glass- and cabinet-maker active in London from the 1690's to the 1720's who was particularly noted for his mirrors (there is one at Hampton Court). Cabinet-maker to George I.

Gun-makers' Marks The testing of barrels to ensure a standard of safety, 'proof-firing', was entrusted to the Gun-makers' Company of London in 1637. There are two kinds of small proof mark, both headed by a crown. The letter 'v' on the first mark means 'viewed after the first test'; the letters 'GP' on the second mark stand for 'Gun-makers' Proof'.

Habaner Ware Broad term that refers to earthenware made by peasant potters of central Europe (Bohemia, Monrovia) in the sixteenth and seventeenth centuries.

Hafner Ware Pottery tiles for stoves made in Germany particularly, but also in Switzerland and France. The making of these tiles specifically for stoves is an ancient craft that goes back to the fourteenth century.

Hague, The A hard-paste porcelain factory founded about 1776 and active until about 1790; the mark is a stork; decorated much porcelain from other factories, notably Tournai.

Hall Chair Formal, upright-backed and square-seated, of mahogany usually; unupholstered; for the caller waiting in the hall.

Hall-mark The particular mark of the Assay Office at which a piece of plate (q.v.) is assayed. Makers' marks and date letters are not, strictly, hall-marks. Hall-marks were introduced in England in 1300 when the Wardens of the London Gold-smiths were ordered to assay and mark with a leopard's head all plate before it left the goldsmith's hands. The purpose was to indicate quality and prevent fraud. In 1363 it was decreed that all goldsmiths should have a mark. At first emblems, these makers' marks became the two first letters of the surname in 1696, and from 1739 onwards they became the initials of Christian and surnames. Date letters were introduced (in London) in 1478. *See* **Britannia** *and* **Sterling Standard.**

The London hall-mark is the leopard's head. Others: Birmingham, an anchor; Sheffield, a crown; Newcastle on Tyne, at first a single castle and then (from about 1672) three castles (the Assay Office closed in 1884); Exeter, a Roman 'x' in various forms at first, then from 1701 a triple-towered castle (Office closed in 1882); Chester, from 1686 three wheat sheaves with a sword, from 1701–80 the three lions of England impaling three wheat sheaves, then three wheat sheaves with a sword again; York, from 1559–1698 the mark has been described as 'half leopard head and half flowre-de-layce', and from 1700 a cross charged with five lions passant (the Office closed in 1857); Norwich, until 1624 a castellated tower over a lion passant guardant, then a rose crowned (Office closed 1697); Edinburgh, a triple-towered castle; Glasgow, tree, fish and bell; Dublin, harp crowned. In some towns silversmiths were allowed to apply town marks themselves; it was customary to use the town arms. Plate so marked has been identified as coming from the following cities and towns: Bristol, Carlisle, Gateshead, Hull, King's Lynn, Leeds, Leicester, Lewes, Lincoln, Poole, Plymouth, Shrewsbury, Taunton.

Hamadan Rugs Persian rugs of rather coarse weave decorated variously in reds, yellows and blues on a buff-coloured ground;

three to four stripe border; woven with the Ghiordiz knot.

Hanap A standing cup (q.v.).

Hanau A famous faience factory founded at Hanau, Hesse, Germany, in 1661 by two Dutchmen who made wares in the Dutch–Chinese manner that can be mistaken for Delft. The factory passed through several hands before its closure about 1806.

Hancock, Robert (1730–1817) Engraver responsible for many of the original engravings for transfer-printing which beautified the porcelains of Bow, Worcester, Caughley, Bristol. He also worked at Battersea where he did engravings for enamels.

Hand-and-cup Vase Small vase of Parian ware, the form being that of a human hand holding aloft a narrow cup.

Handcooler Usually egg-shaped (also called 'eggs'), of hardstone or glass, used for darning.

Han Dynasty (206 B.C. to A.D. 220) *See* **Chinese.**

Harewood Sycamore, stained with a solution of oxide of iron; used as a veneer in the late eighteenth century.

Harpsichord First made in England in the fifteenth century but very few examples survive earlier than the eighteenth century. This stringed musical instrument is enclosed in a case like the later grand piano. It is furnished with two keyboards and extra strings which can be operated by stops. Two great makers in England were Kirkman and Shudi.

Harrison, John (1693–1776) Yorkshire-born clock-maker who invented a marine chronometer and the gridiron pendulum.

Hausmaler (German) An Outside Decorator (q.v.).

Heart Case   Usually of lead or pewter; for the embalming and preserving of a heart bound for a distant burial.

Hedingham   Place-name for pottery made by Edward Bingham at Hedingham, Essex, during the last quarter of the nineteenth century. Bingham produced massive wares, 'Essex' jugs up to three feet high being typical. Hedingham Castle is the usual mark.

Hepplewhite, George (*d*?–. 1786)   English cabinet-maker and designer. Biographical details are few. He was apprenticed to Gillow (q.v.), came later to London and set up in business at St Giles, Cripplegate. He did not achieve any fame in his lifetime as a cabinet-maker. Rather was his reputation procured posthumously by his wife Alice, who continued the business after his death and in 1788 published his *Cabinet Maker and Upholsterers' Guide*. (A third edition, with some alterations, was published in 1794.) In this work the neo-classic style inspired by the brothers Adam (q.v.) is seen with its more conscious classic ornament eliminated or adapted to suit English cabinet-making. Such innovations as the oval, shield and heart-shaped chair back are usually credited to Hepplewhite but there is considerable evidence to suggest that they were not his inventions at all. However, the preface of the *Guide* claims only that it 'followed the latest or most prevailing fashion' and expressly states there had been no intention of originality.

Herculaneum   (1) *Furniture.* According to Sheraton, an upholstered chair in the extreme classical taste. (2) *Pottery.* Earthenware and stoneware, and some unpretentious porcelain, produced at the Herculaneum Pottery, Liverpool, from the 1790's to 1840. Some figures were made but earthenware and stoneware jugs are more typical. The name HERCULANEUM, often wreathed round a crown, is the usual mark.

Hereke Rugs   Silk with Persian patterns, from Hereke on the Sea of Marmora, many-coloured, metallic-laced, as fine as

The Hepplewhite chair

600 knots to square inch. Short-cut pile. Often with the name Hereke in Turkish Arabic on outer stripe.

Herringbone A banding of veneer formed of two strips, of which the grain, running diagonally, produces a herring bone or 'feather' effect.

Highboy Term of comparatively recent origin applied to a chest of drawers resting on a stand or frame.

Hilderson, John Clock-maker active in London in the 1660's and 70's. Very few of his clocks have survived but their quality is high.

Hispano-Moresque Ware Spanish pottery decorated with metallic lustre pigments; the process introduced by the Moors, though it is said to have originated in Persia. Dates from the fourteenth century but most surviving early pieces are not earlier than the fifteenth century.

Höchst A porcelain factory founded at Höchst-am-Main, Germany, under the auspices of the Elector of Mainz, about 1750 and continuing in production until 1798. The mark is a wheel. Faience of good quality was made at Höchst during the period 1746–58. Again the mark is a wheel.

Holdship, Richard and Josiah Part-owners of the Worcester porcelain factory from 1751. Richard Holdship sold his share in 1759 and later offered to sell information regarding the Worcester formula to Duesbury of Derby. Josiah Holdship was perhaps the most important figure in the Worcester partnership until 1762, when Dr Wall took control.

Holland, Henry Architect and designer active 1780–1800 whose work in the classical and the French Directoire styles had a strong influence on his contemporaries. His interiors at Woburn and Southill are notable.

Hollins, Samuel Potter of Shelton, Staffordshire, who produced red and chocolate unglazed ware, also jasper ware, decorated in relief, which is often mistaken for original Elers ware. Hollins was one of the partnership that founded the New Hall porcelain factory.

Hollow Stemmed Drinking Glasses Two brief vogues, mid-Georgian and mid-nineteenth century (where the sediment was supposed to go, but difficult to clean).

Hollow Ware Large pots, tankards, flagons, measures.

Holly A white wood, hard and close-grained, used in marquetry and inlay.

Hood The upper part of a clock case, especially the removable top section of a long-case clock.

Hoof-foot One of the oldest decorative terminals for furniture legs. In England its use dates from the end of the seventeenth century.

Hoop-back Chair back in which the uprights merge into the top rail to form a hoop. The Windsor chair is often a hoop-back.

Hope, Thomas (1769–1831) Author and connoisseur who in 1807 published his *Household Furniture and Interior Decoration* which illustrated the furniture of his Deepdene, Surrey, home. Hope was a designer of considerable talent but his furniture is rather too classical and architectural for most.

Horse Brasses Ornamental brasses used on horse harness; they can be quite valuable if old and genuine, but have sometimes been manufactured lately for use without horses. A few terms: *Face-piece*, amulet worn as a charm against evil either on strap between eyes or on martingale; *Bells*, first hung on harness to warn wayfarers (to fulfil same function as modern motor-horn), they were attached to a swinger which was screwed into a bridle atop the head, with decoration above, often of horse-hair plume or coloured brush; *Brass Rosette*, often in the shape of a cone, worn at end of the brow-band, under the ears, plain or with bells or ribbons suspended; *Martingale*, a strap that extends from belly-band to bridle and particularly decorative, with face-pieces, in the case of cart-horse harness.

Horsehair The use of horsehair (usually mixed with wool) in upholstery dates from the early years of the seventeenth century. Woven hair from the tails and manes of horses, with a cotton or linen warp, was used as a chair covering towards the end of the eighteenth century.

Horseshoe Back Windsor chairs with this shape of back are sometimes so called.

Hutch A term that has been used to indicate quite different articles—a bin or kneading-trough, a dole cupboard (q.v.), a chest, sometimes on legs and sometimes without them and sometimes with canted lid.

Ice-glass Pitted, frosted surface; Venetian originally.

Imari Ware Japanese porcelain from Arita (q.v.) characterized by over-decoration in red, blue and other colours inspired by brocades ('Brocaded Imari'). These wares, which reached England in increasing quantities during the eighteenth century, were copied by many English factories. The Chinese copied them too. Then in the late nineteenth century the Japanese copied themselves—though not very happily—and exported considerable quantities of this product. (Imari was the port a few miles from Arita through which the wares were shipped to Europe.)

Ince (William) and Mayhew (John) Cabinet-makers whose book of designs, the *Universal System of Household Furniture* appeared in parts during the period 1759–63. Their style is a mixture of rococo and Gothic elements in elaborate symmetrical patterns. Ornate chair backs are a feature. Cabinets, stands, mirrors, sconces are frequently decorated with fauna and tendrils.

Incised Decoration Ceramics decoration, the design being executed with a pointed tool, a manner of decorating as old as pottery itself. (*See* **Sgraffito** for a sophisticated variation.)

'India' or 'Indian' Goods Term in use throughout the seventeenth and a good deal of the eighteenth century to describe any articles imported from the Orient.

Inlay (Furniture) A method of decorating furniture by laying small pieces of differently coloured woods (or bone, ivory, etc.) in prepared recesses in the surface of the piece to be decorated. This inlay was a popular form of decoration in the sixteenth and seventeenth centuries on oak and walnut furniture. *See* **Marquetry.**

Intaglio Engraved design which is sunken below the surface— as in glass, ceramics, jewellery.

Intarsia or Tarsia Inlay of coloured woods (or metal, ivory, etc.) much used in Italy in the fifteenth century, particularly on chests. Much esteemed is the work of Fra Giovanno (1459–1525), in which landscapes, vistas of cities and human figures are represented. This form of decoration is the parent of marquetry (q.v.).

Ironstone China Opaque stoneware made first by Spode at the beginning of the nineteenth century and later by several makers, including Mason of Lane Delph and Ridgway of Hanley.

Ispahan Carpets The finest of Persian carpets (the term is often applied to any really fine Persian carpet, regardless of what district it was made in), usually with a wine-red ground and decorated in many colours harmoniously blended. Sixteenth and seventeenth century examples fetch very high prices. (The Ghiordiz knot, usually.)

Istoriato Ceramics painting in which the particular nature of the piece to be decorated tends to be ignored, the ground being treated as though it were a canvas and the subject covering the whole surface of the ware. First used by the Italian maiolica painters in the sixteenth century, the subjects were usually biblical, mythological or historical.

Jackfield The term applies to a black-glazed red earthenware, some of which was made at Jackfield, Shropshire, where potting has been carried out for many centuries.

Jacob, Georges (1739–1814) French cabinet-maker whose chairs are particularly esteemed. He did much work for the Crown.

Jacobite Glasses Drinking glasses bearing propaganda decoration, the significance of which is largely hidden to all but the initiated. Portraits of Bonnie Prince Charlie are readily comprehensible but the Jacobite rose, the butterfly, the stricken and burgeoning oak, etc., are less easily interpreted. These glasses have been faked a lot.

Jacobite Pottery Pottery, salt-glazed stoneware particularlv decorated with Jacobite propaganda (*see* previous entry).

Japanning (Metal) *See* **Pontypool.**

Japanning (Wood) Lacquered or japanned furniture from the Orient began to arrive in England in the second half of the seventeenth century. The best came from Japan. By 1688 Stalker & Parker had brought out their 'do-it-yourself' work, *Treatise of Japanning and Varnishing,* and by the end of the seventeenth century most lacquered furniture was being japanned in England. The ground of the piece to be decorated was coated with layers of 'varnish' and polished when dry. The ornament (in the Oriental style) was drawn on the surface with gold size or vermilion mixed with gum water, and the raised portions put on with a paste composed of whiting and gum arabic. (*See* **Bantam-work** for a note on incised designs.) The taste for japanned furniture extended to the end of the eighteenth century. *See* **Lacquer.**

Jardinière (French)   A pot or other container for flowers.

Jasper Ware   Fine stoneware made by Wedgwood, after experiments, from 1774–5. It contained a substance never before used by a potter, namely barium sulphate. The body was slightly translucent and Wedgwood was able to stain it throughout, first with blue and then with shades of green and then other colours, notably black. Cameos, medallions and plaques were the main products, but vases were also manufactured. 'Jasper dip' was different from 'Jasper solid' in that the body was coloured on the surface only by dipping; this dipped ware is less esteemed.

Jensen, Gerreit (?–1715)   Cabinet-maker who supplied furniture to the Royal Household from the reign of Charles II to that of Queen Anne. Examples of his work that survive prove him to have been a master craftsman—in marquetry, japanned furniture, boulle-work. Mirrors were a speciality.

Jesuit China   Term sometimes applied to Chinese porcelain decorated with religious (Christian) subjects and intended for the European market. Jesuit missionaries were instrumental in bringing about trade between China and the West.

Jew's Porcelain   The Berlin porcelain factory (q.v.) was subsidized in various ways by the ingenious Frederick the Great. One scheme was to force Jews who wished to marry or deal in property to purchase 300 talers' worth of royal porcelain before permission was given. Hence the term.

Johnson, Thomas Furniture designer and noted wood-carver active in London during the third quarter of the eighteenth century. His first book of designs, *Twelve Girandoles*, was published 1755; *One Hundred and Fifty New Designs* came out in parts 1756–8.

Joiner A maker of furniture before the days of the cabinet-maker (who came into his own at the end of the seventeenth century). Originally known as an arkwright, there is a reference to 'the Joyners of the City of London' as early as 1400. The joiner did in fact join pieces of wood together by means of mortise and tenon, dowels or wood pins, whereas the cabinet-maker was to bring with him a new technique which involved the use of different joins and metal fasteners such as nails and screws, also glue.

Jones, Henry (1632–95) Notable English clock-maker; was apprenticed to Edward East in 1654; made clocks and watches of exceptional quality.

Jones, Inigo (1573–1651) Architect who introduced later Italian Renaissance or Palladian work into England during the Jacobean period. It is probable that he personally designed some furniture.

Ju Ware Stoneware of the Sung dynasty comprising a yellowish body and crackled, pale lavender glaze. This ware, which closely approaches porcelain, was made in the early years of the twelfth century; it is very rare and highly esteemed.

Kabistan Rugs Caucasian, of fine weave, making use of the Ghiordiz knot; the wool pile is soft and silky. Designs are usually geometrical, cones, stars, the basic colours being blue and red supported by green, brown and ivory.

Kakiemon A style of decoration that derives from Japanese porcelain—vigorous designs of animals and flowers in bright colours with that asymmetry particular to Japanese art. The

Japanese wares were first imported into Europe from the East by the Dutch in the seventeenth century. The style was much copied by the early European porcelain factories, including such English factories as Chelsea and Worcester. The name comes from a Japanese family of potters who worked at Arita (q.v.).

Kändler, Johann Joachim (1706–75) Porcelain modeller, the foremost such craftsman in the history of European ceramics, appointed chief modeller of the Meissen porcelain factory in 1731, which position he held until his death in 1775. Kändler may be said to have invented the porcelain 'figure' as far as the West is concerned.

Kaolin China clay. *See* **Porcelain.**

Karaja Rugs Persian, of coarse weave and using the Ghiordiz knot, the wool pile being long and lustrous. Blue and red are the basic colours, supported by brown, yellow and white, the favoured decoration being close floral patterns.

Kashan Rugs Persian, of very fine weave, Senna knot, thick, short wool pile. Curved medallions are the usual main design, the floral borders being in red, brown and dark blue with supporting colours. Design of Kashans is particularly graceful; silk examples are to be found. Durability is notable.

Kauffman, Angelica (1741–1807) Swiss painter of Chur and decorative artist who came to London from Venice in 1766. In 1769 she was elected a member of the Royal Academy. She was employed by the brothers Adam to supply decorative paintings, and many painted medallions on contemporary furniture are copied from engravings after her work. She left England in 1782.

Kazak Rugs Caucasian, of coarse weave, Ghiordiz knot, coarse wool pile. Characteristic are the brilliant colours—red, green and yellow supported by blue, brown and white—and large bold patterns of many varieties. The border may have from three to five stripes. Very durable and strong.

Kent, William (1686–1748) Painter, architect, furniture-designer, landscape-gardener—and probably the first English specialist in interior decoration. As a young man he went to Italy to study painting, returning to England in 1719. His first big opportunity came in the early 1720's when he did paintings and decorative work at Kensington Palace. He held a unique position in English art and architecture for the first twenty years of George II's reign. Some examples of his furniture are included in Vardy's *Designs of Inigo Jones and Kent* (1744).

Kelsterbach German hard-paste porcelain factory founded in 1761 with the aid of C. D. Busch who had been at Meissen. Wares of quality were produced until 1768, at which date the factory seems to have ceased production. But in 1789 new staff took over and produced inferior wares until 1802. 'HD', sometimes crowned, is the occasionally encountered mark.

Keshir Rugs A country type of rug from Kir-Shehr, patterned with flowers and geometric forms in red and green and other supporting colours, the light green being predominant and characteristic. Wide borders have a yellow stripe usually. Coarse weft and only thirty to ninety knots to square inch.

Kick The cone, as found in most modern wine bottles, drawn up inside many old glass vessels.

Kidderminster Rugs Kidderminster was probably the first rug-making centre in England, a factory being founded as early as 1735; by *c.* 1750 the first loom for making Brussels carpets was set up and the industry grew to become very prosperous.

Kidney Table Table with top shaped like a kidney; late eighteenth century.

Kingwood Brazilian wood of a rich violet-brown shading into black and showing distinct streaky markings, not unlike Rosewood. It was much used in parquetry and veneer in the late years of the seventeenth century, and again for cross-banding in the second half of the eighteenth century. Also known as *Princewood*—an earlier term.

Kirman Rugs Persian, closely woven, Senna knot, short wool pile; colours are soft—white, pink, grey—and floral and bird patterns are typical.

Kloster-Veilsdorf This German (Thuringian) hard-paste porcelain factory founded in 1760. A monogrammatic 'cv' in various forms is the mark.

Knee The broad upper part of a cabriole leg.

Knee-hole Table Writing tables and dressing tables with recessed centres to accommodate the knees of the sitter date from the early eighteenth century. By the second half of the eighteenth century the Library table with matching pedestals (containing drawers) at each end had evolved from the knee-hole table.

Knibbs, The A family of English clock-makers. The earliest of whom records exist was Samuel Knibb of Claydon, Oxon., who worked in London from 1663 to about 1670. His cousin, Joseph Knibb, also of Claydon, was one of the greatest English clock-makers. He came to London *c.* 1670 and worked there till 1697; he introduced 'Roman striking' in England, also (perhaps) night clocks. His brother, John, was another gifted clock-maker; worked at Oxford but continued to collaborate with Joseph when the latter came to London. Peter and Edward were younger members of this clock-wise family.

Knife Box or Case A case with its interior divided into small compartments in which knives and forks and spoons were inserted, the knives and forks handles upwards, the spoons bowls upwards. The sloping top and serpentine front are usual till the second half of the eighteenth century when a new type was introduced. This new type was of vase form and the partitions were arranged round a central tube or stem to which the lid or cover was attached. The lid could be kept up, when required, by means of a spring. These 'knife-vases' were often made in pairs.

Knop Archaic for *knob*, a disc, bulge or swelling, the usage being mainly confined to such decoration on glass stems. The principal types are as follows (only the first few are described; the remainder are self-explanatory). *Annulated*, flattened, with similar, progressively smaller, matching knops above and below it; *bladed*, flattened and sharp-edged; *bullet*, small, globular; *cushion*, largish, spherical but flattened at top and bottom; *cusped*, with an often irregular edge where fluting or facet-cutting from above and below meet at the widest point of the knop; *drop*, inverted conc; *merese* (or *collar*), flat, like a button; *quatrefoil*, with four wings or lobes, pinched into shape. The others: acorn (which may be inverted), angular, ball, beaded, bobbin, button, compressed ball, cone, cylinder, dumb-bell, egg, melon, mushroom, triple ring (the simplest form of the annulated), urn-shaped. There are many, many combinations of the knopped stem. Of interest is the knop with a coin enclosed; examples have been found with coins dating from the late seventeenth century, but the coin is all too likely to be older than the glass.

Knulling *See* **Gadrooning.**

Konieh Rugs From the Whirling Dervish city of Konieh, ancient Iconium, with many geometric and floral designs in rich colours, notably red and blue; coarse weave.

Ko Ware Stoneware of the Sung dynasty comprising a dark body and variously shaded grey glaze with a fine-meshed crackle. Similar to *Kuan Ware* (q.v.).

Krater (Greek) Vase-shaped vessel with two handles.

109

Ku (Chinese) Ancient, slender, bronze wine vessel greatly esteemed for its proportions; not unlike an upturned trumpet, it has a base about half the diameter of the mouth, a slender knop and a wide, flaring mouth. The design was copied by Chinese makers of porcelain in the late Ming and early Ch'ing periods.

Kuan Ware Stoneware of the Sung dynasty comprising a dark grey body and thick greyish-green or greyish-blue glaze which usually has an irregular crackle. Made early in the twelfth century at K'ai-feng-fu and then at Hang-chou. Very rare and much esteemed.

Kuei (Chinese) Ancient bronze bowl, deep, low, often with convex sides and usually with two handles.

Kulah Rugs Turkish rug noted for its fine floral borders; mostly prayer rugs; coarse.

Kurdish Rugs Rather vague term for colourful rugs made by nomadic tribesmen of Kurdistan.

Kutani Porcelain Porcelain made at this Japanese factory since the mid-seventeenth century; 'Old Kutani', brilliantly coloured in Prussian blue, green, yellow and purple, as made until *c*. 1750, is much esteemed.

Kyoto Japanese ceramics-making centre in Yamashiro Province. Pottery made until the eighteenth century, then both pottery and porcelain; the best of the latter was made in imitation of Sung celadons.

Laburnum Hard wood of yellowish tint streaked with brown, used for parquetry veneer from the end of the seventeenth century.

Lace Glass *Vetro de trina*, the finest work in the *latticino* (q.v.) technique.

110

Lacquer   The art of lacquering (which was known in China as early as the middle of the first millennium B.C.) originated in the discovery of the protective properties of the sap of the lac-tree (*Rhus vernicifera*) which can be used to coat almost any material and forms a hard semi-transparent film. Chinese lacquering falls into three groups: (1) the ornament raised in low relief; (2) painted upon the surface, and (3) cut or incised. The trade in Chinese lacquered goods was extensive in the early eighteenth century and patterns of cabinet work were sent out to China in the reign of Charles II to teach the Chinese what manufactured goods were required for the English market. *See* **Japanning.**

Ladder-back   Chair-back with horizontal rails like a ladder, though the rails were usually curved. Popular in the middle years of the eighteenth century.

Ladik Rugs   The old Laodicea is now the village Ladik where these rugs with hexagonal medallions and vandyke end-panels are made in red and blue and supporting colours. Medium weave.

Lambeth   Loosely used term for tin-enamelled earthenware (*delft*, q.v.) as made at Lambeth, Southwark and other London riverside potworks in the seventeenth and eighteenth centuries.

Lambrequin (French)   A design, generally with a shaped or scalloped edge, which may be painted, chased or engraved; sometimes taking the form of a piece of drapery, it can also be imitative of lace or wrought-iron decoration.

Lamerie, Paul de (?–1751)   Huguenot silversmith who worked in London from *c.* 1712 and taught English silversmiths much of the rococo while producing silver wares of great beauty and value.

Lancashire Chair   An oak type, with solid back panel surmounted by lunette-shaped cresting.

Langley, Batty and Thomas The Langley brothers, designers and architects, published in 1740 a work entitled *The City and Country Builder's and Workman's Treasury of Designs*, which included furniture designs in the French manner.

Langlois, Peter French cabinet-maker who worked in London in the 1760's, specializing in inlaid work 'in the politest manner'. Horace Walpole was a customer.

Lantern Clock Earliest type of domestic clock in general use in England. *See* **Clocks.**

Larch The wood of this conifer is hard and tough and the grain is straight, but it warps badly and for this reason it was seldom used in furniture-making. It was, however, employed for carcase work in the late eighteenth century.

Latten A base yellow alloy of zinc and copper; like brass.

Lattice-work Furniture (chairs particularly) of the mid-eighteenth century in the Chinese taste made use of lattice-work decoration. *See* **Fretwork.**

Latticinio or Latticino A glass decorating technique, of Venetian origin, though the Romans had something very like it. The process, at its simplest for drinking glass stems, involved placing opaque and/or coloured canes in a mould into which clear glass was poured. After fusion and cooling the resultant rod could be reheated and stretched to the thickness of a glass stem, the enclosed canes becoming mere threads. Twisting supplied a spiral. The same basic process in more complicated forms was applied to vases and plates, for which the threads were tooled into a network and melted into the surface of the clear ware. Long in favour—sixteenth to eighteenth centuries—and revived most successfully, at Nailsea particularly, during the nineteenth century.

Leather Leather-covered furniture figures widely in the inventories of the sixteenth century. For Cromwellian chairs a favoured covering was leather fastened with brass-headed nails. Later came painted and gilded leather and about 1750 red morocco as a chair covering was in use. Generally speaking leather was employed on chairs that were made for hard usage. Leather hangings, popular in some Continental countries such as Spain, never seem to have found much favour in England.

Le Brun, Charles (1619–90) Foremost among the artists patronized by Louis XIV, responsible for the decoration of the Gallery of Apollo in the Louvre and director of Gobelins tapestry manufactory in its first and greatest period.

Leeds The most important of the Yorkshire potteries, the factory founded about 1760 by the Green brothers, to be known from the mid-1770's as Humble, Green & Co., by the end of the century as Hartley, Greens & Co., and trading under several names and ownerships from 1820 till its close in 1878. Leeds is best known for its creamware, particularly pierced work at which the factory was pre-eminent, but various types of earthenware and stoneware were made, including Wedgwood-like black basalts. Marks usually comprised the name of the firm.

Lei (Chinese) Ancient bronze vessel, intended for wine, ovoid in shape, often with a looped handle.

Leleu, M. J. F. French eighteenth-century cabinet-maker who worked under Oeben (q.v.).

Lenticle The 'porthole' in the trunk of a long-case clock through which the pendulum bob can be seen.

Li (Chinese) Udder-shaped cooking vessel probably first evolved in Neolithic pottery; the bronze *li* is considered the earliest of all Chinese metal vessels; stands on three feet usually.

Library Chair Chairs made specifically for reading in the library date from the early eighteenth century. The top rail curves round to become an arm-rest from which a canted board angles up and back to afford a rest for book or writing paper, and the reader sits back to front in the chair. A Library or Reading chair of the Regency period was more likely to be caned, with removable leather-covered cushions, and to have an adjustable book-rest attached to one arm.

Library Steps Date from about the middle of the eighteenth century. Folding steps, in combination with chairs, tables, and the like, are often very ingenious as regards their construction.

Library Table A writing-table, especially one of twin-pedestal type, specifically made for the library from the middle of the eighteenth century. A distinct type, circular or square, supported by a single pedestal with winged legs, and having space in the frieze for books (a single shelf right round the table in fact), was made at the end of the eighteenth century.

Lignum Vitae A West Indian wood, dark brown with strong veining and streaked with black. Imported into England during the seventeenth and eighteenth centuries. Very hard. Used as parquetry and in veneering.

Lille Porcelain A soft-paste porcelain factory was founded at Lille, France, about 1711 and continued in production until 1730, although production seems to have been small and examples are rare. A hard-paste factory was established about

Lille china marks

1784 and lasted until the early years of the nineteenth century. This factory, the first in France to use coal for firing, had an appointment to the *Dauphin*, hence its mark, a crowned dolphin.

114

Limbach Porcelain   A porcelain factory founded at Limbach, Thuringia, Germany, about 1772 by Gotthelf Greiner for the production of useful wares that have little artistic merit. The Greiner family established several factories in Thuringia—at Grossbreitenbach, Ilmenau, Gera, Rauenstein.

Lime   A wood of light straw colour with close, compact grain; easy to work and much favoured for ornamental carving.

Limehouse   There was a porcelain factory in this district of London *c.* 1747 but its life was a short one and no wares have been definitely attributed to it.

Limoges Enamel   The French town of Limoges was a famous centre of enamelling in medieval times and developed a trade that covered Europe. Painted enamels of the sixteenth century are superb.

Limoges Porcelain   The first porcelain factory at Limoges, France, was founded in 1771, purchased by the King in 1784 and for a time served as a branch of Sèvres. A number of porcelain factories were founded at and near Limoges during the nineteenth century owing to the *kaolin* deposits in the area.

Linenfold Pattern   The decorative device for panel enrichment (variously termed *drapery* and *parchment-scroll* pattern) appears in the carved work of French and Flemish artists about the middle of the fifteenth century. The resemblance to folded linen is very slight in early examples, but later variations show a tendency towards complexity and the upper and lower edges are sometimes fantastically cut and shaped. The vogue in England lasted from the last quarter of the fifteenth century to the middle of the sixteenth.

Linen-press   A device for pressing linen. The structure comprises a frame and base board, and a matching top board which was attached to a wooden, spiral screw. Examples from the seventeenth century survive.

Ling Lung Chinese porcelain bowl or dish with pierced sides.

Linnell, John (?–1796) Cabinet-maker, designer, carver, who supplied many noted figures of his day with furniture in the Chinese and rococo styles then prevalent. Many of his designs are in the Victoria and Albert Museum, London.

Lion's Mask Decoration used by furniture-makers (particularly on the knees of cabriole legs) from about 1720 to 1740 and again during the Regency. This motif was also used by metalworkers.

Lithography The printing process, based on the antipathy of grease and water, invented in the late eighteenth century by Senefelder, first used as a form of transfer-printing on ceramics in England about 1840 but never very successfully until the present century.

Lithophane A plaque of porcelain or bone china, very thin, bearing a design or picture engraved, and meant to be viewed against a light; nineteenth century.

Littler, William Eighteenth-century Staffordshire potter noted for his salt-glazed stoneware, produced at Brownhills, near Burslem, and for the porcelain made at Longton Hall (q.v.), the factory he founded about 1750. Littler is credited with the introduction of cobalt blue to Staffordshire.

Liverpool Considering the amount of ceramics produced at and near Liverpool extraordinarily few facts are known. It was certainly an early centre for delftware, the manufacture of which was in decline by the last quarter of the eighteenth century. But earthenware of all kinds was made throughout the eighteenth century and it is probable that the export trade to America was much larger than is generally realized. The making of porcelain probably dates from the 1750's and it is considered that there were a number of small factories engaged in its manufacture. The only factory of which even a little is

known is that of Richard Chaffers, who made a porcelain containing soaprock which resembles early Worcester. Decoration
is in the Chinese manner. The factory is thought to have been
active 1756–65. John Sadler of Liverpool, in partnership with
Guy Green, was one of the earliest to use transfer-printing; he
may even have invented the process in the early 1750's.

Livery Cupboard A cupboard which during the sixteenth
century and the first half of the seventeenth century served to
contain 'liveries' (consisting of food, drink and candles) given
out at night-time to members of a household, and guests.

Lobby Chest Diminutive chest of drawers.

Lobing *See* **Gadrooning.**

Locking Plate Striking System in a clock of striking the hours
and sometimes the half-hours by means of a locking wheel or
plate in which notches are cut, the notches being farther and
farther apart from the one o'clock position round to the
twelve o'clock position. Dates from about 1625 but was ousted
in the late 1670's by Barlow's rack and snail striking (q.v.).

Lock, Matthias Carver and designer of whom little is known.
He was active 1740–70 and during that time he published
several works of furniture designs (some in collaboration with
a colleague named Copland) whose titles usually began *A New
Book of Ornaments.* . . . It is thought now that Lock and
Copland deserve a good deal of the credit for translating the
French rococo style into English terms as regards furniture
making, and, moreover, they seem to have been the draughts-
men who did many of the plates in Chippendale's *Director*.

Locks The lock was probably an Egyptian invention that
goes back more than 4,000 years. 'Warded' locks (i.e. a lock
with a fixed obstruction to prevent the wrong key from enter-
ing) are very old; superb examples were made in medieval
times. Next comes the 'tumbler' lock, which differs from the

ward in that the obstruction moves when the right key is inserted. The tumbler lock is thought to have been a Chinese invention. Another basic form of lock is the combination or 'letter' lock in which the letters of the alphabet are engraved on revolving rings (four usually), the mechanism being set to permit the lock to open only if the correct combination is known.

For domestic locks the two basic actions are the bolt and the latch. The bolt slides horizontally to engage in a plate or catch in the door jamb; the latch is hinged at one end, the other, free end engaging in a catch on the door jamb. The lock protected by a metal case dates back (in England) to the early sixteenth century. By the second half of the seventeenth century these cases were the subject of engraved and pierced decoration of great skill and richness.

The mortise lock came into use in the middle of the eighteenth century and brought with it another kind of door furniture, this being the plate to accommodate the door handle, the escutcheon and (sometimes) a smaller handle to operate the bolt.

Long-case Clock The correct name for a grandfather clock; first made *c.* 1660.

Long Elizas (from the Dutch *Lange Lyzen*) The elongated Chinese girls on Chinese porcelains, copied by English eighteenth-century makers, especially Worcester.

Longton Hall Facts about this porcelain factory, probably the first established in Staffordshire, are elusive. It seems to have been founded in 1751 by a partnership of which the

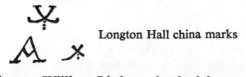

Longton Hall china marks

leading spirit was William Littler, who had been engaged in the manufacture of salt-glazed stoneware at Brownhills, the style of the firm being Littler & Co. The factory closed in (perhaps before) 1760. Two types of soft-paste porcelain were made. The first is crude, rather heavy, with 'moons' often and with an uneven surface; dishes in the form of leaves are typical. Later a somewhat finer ware was produced which approaches Chelsea in quality. Longton Hall figures are esteemed and much sought by collectors. Crossed 'L's' are the usual mark.

Loo Table   Folding card table; sometimes baize-topped; name derives from game of 'Loo'.

Lopers   Slides to support drop-fronts of bureaux.

Louis XIV, Style of   The period between 1660 and 1715, known as the *Grand Siècle* and characterized by State intervention in the production of works of art. Decoration was sumptuous and massive; much use was made of modelled stucco, gilt metal ornaments and marble for wall-linings. Metal marquetry was developed by Boulle (q.v.).

Louis XV, Style of (1723–74)   After a short period of transition (*see* **Régence**) the style shows a greater suppleness in the general design of decoration and furniture, a reaction against the preceding reign. The rococo (q.v.) was established with its accent on asymmetry. Seat furniture became lighter and more comfortable, and small bureaux and tables were designed.

Louis XVI, Style of (1744–93)   During this period the straight line was recalled to structure in furniture and decoration. Under the influence of the classical revival vertical and horizontal lines predominate and detail moves in the direction of refinement and delicacy until about 1790.

Love-seat   A small settee for two and no more.

Loving Cup   Twin-handled drinking vessel.

Lowboy American term for a small dressing table with drawers; often made *en suite* with the highboy (q.v.).

Lowestoft This porcelain factory founded in 1757 and continued in production till about 1800. The Bow-like paste contains bone-ash. Under-glaze blue was the favoured decoration and the Chinese influence is obvious. Small pieces, souvenirs for visitors ('A Trifle from Lowestoft'), were made in considerable quantity. There is no Lowestoft mark as such, but the marks of several factories were used, especially Worcester. 'Oriental Lowestoft' is, of course, a complete misnomer as applied to porcelain made in China for the European market and has nothing to do with this factory.

Ludwigsburg A hard-paste porcelain factory founded about 1758 by the Duke of Württemberg. J. J. Ringler, who had been at Vienna and other factories, was Director from 1759 till

Ludwigsburg china marks

about 1800. The factory closed in 1824. Some of the figures made here are greatly esteemed and fetch very high prices. The early mark, which covers the best period, comprises two c's linked back to back, sometimes surmounted by a crown.

Lunette Half-moon.

Lung-Ch'üan Ware Celadon ware from the ceramics centre of Lung-Ch'üan, Chekiang Province, China, where stoneware and porcelain were produced from as early as the ninth century. The term covers various types of ware, the finest being a thinly-potted stoneware with a pale green glaze made during the Sung dynasty. More common is a heavier stoneware with a glaze in various shades of green that often approximate jade.

Lustre *Glass*. Originally a chandelier, a lustre is now usually a vase with flaring rim from which hang prismatic glass pendants; candle lustres are candle stands with hanging glass pendants. *Ceramics*. Pottery and sometimes porcelain covered with a thin coating of metal. The process is very old. Hispano-Moresque ware (q.v.) is lustre, for example. The metal most commonly used in England was copper, with platinum ('silver') next and then gold. There are several methods of application but the two main classifications are Painted Lustres in which the pottery is completely covered with the metal, and Resist Lustres in which over-glaze painting is combined with the metallic decoration.

Lyre-back Chair back in which the back is carved in the shape of a lyre (late eighteenth century).

Mahogany Three varieties of mahogany were used in the eighteenth century. 'Spanish' (or 'St Domingo') was used from about 1725 to about 1750, when the 'Cuban' and then the 'Honduras' varieties came into use. Some of the Cuban timber is finely figured and marked with a curly or wavy grain. The Honduras timber is generally inferior in colour and figure to the other two, but it is lighter in weight and softer in texture. From the point of view of design, mahogany was responsible for two main innovations. One was that the great width of the boards enabled table tops, for instance, to be made in one or two sections instead of several (as was necessary with walnut); the other was that the great strength of mahogany permitted slender and delicate work (fretwork, splatwork, etc.). Mahogany remained in popular use well into the nineteenth century. The 'age of mahogany' 1720–70.

Maigelein Early German drinking glass in the form of a low palm cup (without handles) and with a 'kick' (a cone of glass drawn up inside—as with many modern wine bottles).

Maiolica   Earthenware with a tin-enamel glaze as made in Italy in the fifteenth, sixteenth, seventeenth and eighteenth centuries. The sixteenth century was the great age of maiolica. The name is said to derive from the island of Majorca, whence Spanish lustre-ware was exported to Italy. Painted decoration consisted mainly of cobalt blue, yellow, purple, green and iron red, together with combinations of these. The use of lustre was an important development, as was the *istoriato* (q.v.) style of painting. Of the many Italian maiolica centres Faenza (*see* **Faience**) was one of the earliest and most important; others were Forli, Siena, Orvieto, Florence, Ravenna, Deruta, Urbino, Castel Durante.

Majolica   This term so spelt was given to pottery decorated in relief beneath a coloured glaze and manufactured at various English factories in the second half of the nineteenth century.

Makri Rugs   Made in coastal districts across from the Island of Rhodes, and exceedingly rare, with their end arches and fields divided into coloured panels, and their bright eight-pointed stars, leaves, latch-hooks. Red, blue, yellow, green and white. Coarsely woven with forty-five to sixty-five knots to the square inch.

Malling Jugs   Tin-enamelled pottery jugs, globular in shape, as made, probably in London, in the sixteenth and seventeenth centuries; these jugs, with their splashed or mottled glaze, are the earliest known examples of delftware (q.v.) in England. The name derives from West Malling, Kent, where one of the first specimens was found.

Manheim Gold   Alloy of copper, zinc and tin.

Manton, Joseph   Late eighteenth- and early nineteenth-century British gunsmith deemed one of the greatest gun-makers of all time. His improvements to the flintlock included the elevated rib above the barrel, the gravitating stop, and the recessed double breech. Many features of the double-barrelled shotgun have not changed since Manton's time. His brother, John, was also a great gunsmith.

Manwaring, Robert   Chair-maker and author of *The Cabinet and Chair Maker's Real Friend and Companion* (1765).

Maple   This indigenous tree is often called sycamore in England and plane tree in Scotland. The white wood takes a good polish. It was used in marquetry and as veneer in the seventeenth and eighteenth centuries. The 'bird's eye' maple is an American wood (the sugar maple), and much superior with its fine grain and texture and figuring.

Marble Tops   Marble slabs for table tops were in use in the sixteenth century but it was not till the early years of the eighteenth century that they became at all common in England. Though marble was quarried in England most slabs for use with furniture were imported from Italy and the Englishman of the eighteenth century making the Grand Tour would look for a choice slab as he would for choice pictures. *See* **Scagliola.**

Marbling   (1) Wood treated to look like marble had a vogue at the end of the sixteenth century and the beginning of the seventeenth. For veneer, holly burrs cut from the trunks of old trees and then stained were used with other coloured woods, more straight-forward was the 'marbling' of panelling and fireplace surrounds by painting the wood. (2) Marbled slipware decoration on English pottery was popular in the eighteenth century (Chinese potters practised it during the T'ang and Sung dynasties) and consists of combing 'slips' of contrasting colours to produce the appearance of natural marble.

Marieberg   Swedish (Stockholm) ceramics factory which produced faience from about 1760, soft-paste porcelain from about 1766 (when Pierre Berthevin from Mennecy (q.v.) became manager), and some hard-paste porcelain from about 1777. The factory closed in 1788. Particularly admired are the small well-modelled creampots with covers, fluted spirals and delicately painted bouquets of flowers; also the statuettes and the rococo candelabra. The most common mark is 'MB'.

Marot, Daniel (?1660–1720?)   French architect and furniture-designer who entered the service of William, Prince of Orange, and later accompanied him to England, where he worked for a few years in the 1690's. His designs for furniture and complete interiors in the Louis XIV style had a considerable influence on his contemporaries.

Marquetry   The process of cutting, fitting and inlaying veneers of various light-coloured woods in a darker veneer ground for application to the carcase of a piece of furniture. This form of furniture decoration was first used in England in the 1670's. Floral marquetry was in vogue at first but towards the end of the seventeenth century and in the early years of the eighteenth century a type of veneer in which two contrasting woods only were used, called arabesque or seaweed marquetry, came into fashion. A revival of marquetry took place in the second half of the eighteenth century. *See* **Inlay.**

Marquise (French)   A small sofa; a love-seat.

Marsh, William   Cabinet-maker and upholsterer to the Prince of Wales (later George IV); Marsh and his partners supplied furniture for Carlton House and the Brighton Pavilion.

Mary Gregory Glass   Coloured (dark blue, ruby, amber, green) ware, usually with white enamelled brush-work figures of children at play or flower paintings. Of Bohemian origin but now bears name of American artist famous, in the nineteenth century, for portraits of children on glass.

Mason   Family of potters active during the first half of the nineteenth century. The father, Miles Mason, probably worked at Liverpool before setting up a porcelain factory at

Fenton in about 1800; William, Charles and George are the other members of the family which made an extremely hard porcelain, 'ironstone china', bone-china and earthenware. The Chinese manner of decoration was much favoured. Enormous vases are typical. Apart from the names 'Mason' and 'Fenton', the usual mark is a crown.

Matchlock The earliest form of gun ignition, probably invented during the second quarter of the fifteenth century, perhaps at Nuremberg, it consisted of an S-shaped piece of iron pivoting on its side which when swivelled inserted a glowing fuse into a powder-filled touch-hole.

Matt A rough surface. The term is sometimes applied to an unpolished or unfinished area of a metal object, but as regards silver, much seventeenth-century silverware was decorated by burring with a metal punch to produce a matt surface.

Mayhew, Thomas *See* **Ince and Mayhew.**

Mazarine Originally a bowl or cup, but now a pierced silver dish used as a strainer for fish dishes.

Mazer Broad bowl of maple wood sometimes mounted on and/or with silver or pewter. Last made in the sixteenth century.

Medallion A circular or oval disc decorated with objects in relief; also a portion of a decorative design (as in carpets) which is specially treated.

Meigh Family of potters active at Hanley from the late eighteenth century; best known are the jugs they made under the influence of the Gothic revival in the middle of the nineteenth century.

Mei Ping (Chinese) A form of Chinese porcelain vase with squat body, small neck and mouth, supposedly intended to hold a single spray of the prunus blossom and for this reason sometimes called 'prunus vase'.

Meissen Europe's first and most important hard-paste porcelain manufactory, situated some twelve miles from Dresden, Saxony, Germany, founded in 1710 and named the Royal Saxon Porcelain Manufacture. The first years were largely experimental. Two classes of ware were made, true porcelain and red stoneware, both the invention of J. F. Böttger (q.v.). By about 1714 the factory was in commercial production. Böttger died in 1719 and the venture might well have collapsed had not the King (Augustus the Strong, Elector of Saxony and King of Poland) appointed a Commission to reorganize and enlarge the factory. Progress was almost uninterrupted from 1720 to 1756 (the year the Seven Years War broke out); a disturbed period followed and by the time the factory management was reconstituted (1763–4) Meissen faced serious competition from other European factories, particularly from Sèvres. The so-called 'Academic Period' followed (1763–74) and then came the period of Marcolini's management (1774–1814). In the nineteenth century the decline was unspectacular.

Until 1733: Shapes at first followed those of contemporary baroque silver. Painted decoration was undistinguished until 1720 when Johann Gregor Herold, enameller and miniaturist, came to Meissen. As Art Director, Herold was responsible for painted decoration and the colours evolved and he soon gave the factory a brilliant palette. Underglaze blue, though never particularly successful at Meissen, dates from about 1725, as do most of the famous ground colours, yellow, blue, green, lilac, grey, crimson-purple. Some of the finest painted decoration was done in the Chinese and Japanese styles; but landscapes and harbour scenes are also notable. Figures were made, animals, grotesque human figures such as dwarfs, but this was the great period of painted decoration; modelling came into its own with the advent of Kändler.

1733–63: Johann Joachim Kändler (q.v.) came to Meissen in 1731 and was appointed chief modeller in 1733. With him the baroque (although by this time giving way to the rococo) found expression in terms of porcelain. He almost invented the 'figure' and that it later became the 'Dresden figure' was no fault of his. He drew inspiration from many and diverse sources and his figures range from Harlequin to street trader, shepherdess to artisan, gallant to Olympian god, court lady to monkey band. His earliest work is his best. Though he adapted himself to the rococo style he was never happy in it.

Modelled and moulded relief decoration was introduced to table wares and vases. Scrolls and basketwork patterns became more and more elaborate as the influence of the rococo style grew stronger. What began as border decoration (on plates, for example) spread over the entire surface. Moulded flowers had a vogue; the lips and handles of jugs and coffee-pots carried scrolls and flourishes. Tureens in the form of vegetables and animals were made in the 1740's and 50's.

As regards painted decoration, *chinoiseries* remained popular. Formal Oriental flower patterns had a vogue until *c.* 1740, when more naturalistic European flower painting came into favour. At about this time, too, pastoral scenes deriving from Watteau and other French painters were introduced, and later, in the 1750's, mythological subjects.

1764–74: The Academic Period. Michel-Victor Acier, a French sculptor, was appointed chief modeller, jointly with Kändler, in 1764. Herold retired in 1765. The old order was giving way to a new neo-classicism. Symmetry, and rather stiff symmetry at that, replaced the rococo curve. Painted decoration became more and more naturalistic. The prevailing styles of Sèvres were followed. Lace decoration (lace dipped in slip and then applied to a figure; during firing the material burned away leaving the mesh design on the ware) dates from *c.* 1770. This was all very well but, clearly, the great days were over.

1774–1814: Count Camillo Marcolini was appointed Director in 1774. He did what he could to revive Meissen's prosperity, but circumstances (not least in the form of Wedgwood's wares) were against him. The Thuringian factories imitated (and under-cut) Meissen; Meissen imitated Sèvres. Topographical decoration was good but uninspired. The financial position the factory was precarious; Marcolini sold much defective white porcelain that had accumulated over the years in order to raise money.

The nineteenth century: The classical style lasted until about 1830. The influence of Wedgwood is to be discerned. Lithophanes (q.v.) were a popular novelty introduced in 1828. The rococo style was revived between 1835–70 and Dresden figures were produced in enormous numbers. The export trade to England and the United States in the second half of the nineteenth century was big business. Most of the 'Dresden' china to be found in antique shops today is late nineteenth century. (Many experts apply the term 'Meissen' to eighteenth-century products of this factory, and the term 'Dresden' to wares produced after 1800.)

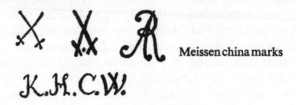

Meissen china marks

Crossed swords are the famous mark, first used about 1724. A dot between the hilts signifies the Academic Period; a star between the hilts was applied during the Marcolini management.

Melas Rugs From south-west Asia Minor, with narrow fields and broad main stripes. Red, yellow, ivory, blue, mauve; and coarsely loose with sixty to eighty Ghiordiz knots to the square inch.

Mendelsham Chair A type of Windsor chair as made at Mendlesham in Suffolk in the early nineteenth century. The back usually has a straight top rail and a narrow upright splat.

Mennecy Soft-paste porcelain made at this factory between 1735 and 1785, at first in the style of Saint-Cloud and later in the style of Sèvres. Kakiemon patterns are a feature of early wares. The factory transferred to Bourg-la-Reine in 1773. The usual mark is 'DV'.

Menuisier French term that corresponds to the English 'carpenter'. One who worked in plain or carved woods lacking veneers for furniture, also timber and panelling for the building of houses.

Meshed Rugs Persian rugs usually incorporating a large central medallion and floral designs; red, blue and white are the principal colours supported by yellows and greens; multi-striped (as many as eight) border; Senna knot usually.

Mezza-Maiolica A misnomer (the term means half-maiolica) sometimes applied to lead-glazed earthenware decorated in the *sgraffito* (q.v.) technique.

Mikawachi Japanese ceramics factory which made porcelain of fine quality from the middle of the eighteenth century.

Millefiori (Italian = 'a thousand flowers') The term applies to a technique of Roman glass mosaic in which bundles of slender glass rods of varied colours were fused together in a cylinder which was drawn out while still plastic and afterwards cut into transverse sections. The process was revived by Venetian glass-makers in the fifteenth and sixteenth centuries, and again in France and England in the nineteenth century. *See* **Paper-weight.**

Ming Dynasty (A.D. 1368–1644) *See* **Chinese.**

Minton The factory founded by Thomas Minton in 1796. At first pottery only was made but soft-paste porcelain was produced probably as early as 1798. In 1817 Minton took his sons into the business and the firm traded as Thomas Minton & Sons. The father died in 1836 and John Boyle entered the firm which then became known as Minton & Boyle until 1845 brought a new partner, Michael Hollins, and a new style, Minton Hollins & Co. In 1883 the present style of Mintons Ltd was adopted.

Porcelain was not produced in any great quantity at Minton in its early years, but about 1825 several Derby artists took employment with the firm and output—and quality—increased. Sèvres provided a recurring inspiration which extended to the marking of many pieces. Parian ware was a noted product from about 1845; and Marc-Louis Solon, who had been with Sèvres, introduced the celebrated *pâte-sur-pâte* technique. It is generally agreed that Minton made some of the best porcelain produced in England during the Victorian period—and indeed they still produce porcelain of fine quality.

    Minton china marks

Marks include the letter 'm', the Sèvres-like mark, the name 'Minton' impressed or transfer-printed.

Miquelet Lock An early form of flintlock (q.v.) developed in Spain perhaps as early as 1587.

Mirrors In ancient China and in classical antiquity mirrors were of polished metal. This was still generally so in the Middle Ages in Europe, for, though the method of backing glass with a metallic substance to make it reflect was known, the imperfections and distortions due to impurities in the glass ruled out a satisfactory reflection. Hand mirrors of gold, silver or bronze, enriched with precious stones, were the treasured possessions of the very wealthy in medieval times. By the fifteenth century mirrors were usually of steel or crystal. Venetian glass-makers claimed to have perfected glass mirrors in 1507; this was a monopoly they held for a long time but by the early seventeenth century craftsmen from Murano (near

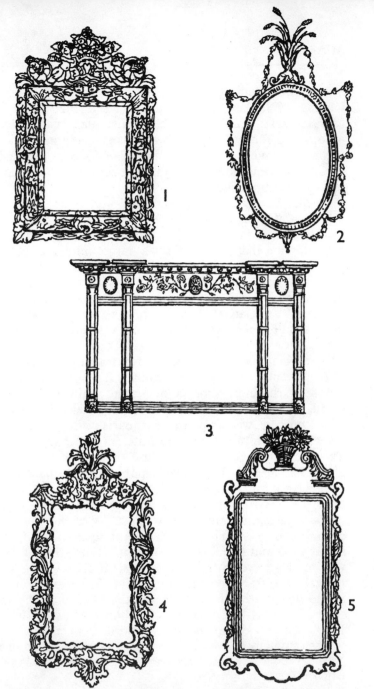

The mirror. 1, *c.* 1675 (Charles II). 2, *c.* 1780 (Adam). 3, *c.* 1820 (Regency). 4, *c.* 1765 (Chippendale). 5, *c.* 1750

Venice) were coming to England to instruct the natives in the making of looking-glass plates. By the 1620's Sir Robert Mansell (*see* **Glass**) had got the English glass-making industry on a sound footing, mirrors were being made in considerable quantities, and hanging mirrors began to play a part in the decorative domestic scheme of things. A considerable manufacture was set up at Vauxhall *c.* 1665.

During these early years mirrors were made from blown cylinders of glass that were slit open, flattened and polished, and the backs silvered with tin and mercury. It is worth remembering that in the 1670's a 'large' mirror would not be more than three feet in length. By the 1680's the English were claiming they made the best mirrors in the world; by the beginning of the eighteenth century foreigners were beginning to agree. The relatively low cost of the English product during the first half of the eighteenth century was a factor that amazed the visitor.

Many materials were used for frames from the last quarter of the seventeenth century: various soft woods that lent themselves to carvings, veneers of walnut, laburnum and olive wood, marquetry, japanned woods, tortoiseshell, ivory, silver. Most mirrors were square or squarish till the end of the seventeenth century when the taste for tall mirrors came in. This greater height meant the use of two or more plates of glass. The arched crest became popular. Overmantel mirrors grew larger and larger. The pier glass (tall and narrow to occupy the space between windows) came in at the beginning of the eighteenth century and was usually of carved wood gilt, decorated in gesso. The architectural style of mirror dates from about 1725 and remained in vogue until the straight line gave way to the curve in the 1740's. Thereafter (until the classical revival) the frame-maker could give full expression to his virtuosity, whether in the rococo, the Gothic or the Chinese styles. The classical influence of Adam made itself felt in the 1760's and was dominant till the end of the century.

The circular convex mirror became popular in England about 1800 (they had been made much earlier in France, whence the fashion came).

Modillion Series of projecting brackets below the cornice or in the pediment—as found on eighteenth-century furniture designed in the architectural manner.

Mohair Strictly, a fine camlet made from the hair of the Angora goat; but the term was used in the seventeenth and eighteenth centuries to denote a kind of silk used for upholstery and hangings.

Mongol or Yüan Dynasty (A.D. 1279–1368) *See* **Chinese.**

Monks' Bench Combined table, settle and chest.

Monopodium Solid three- or four-sided table pedestal, often mounted on feet, popular during the Regency.

Monstrance Vessel, often of silver or gold and richly decorated, in which the Host is exposed.

Monteith Punch bowl with scalloped rim which is frequently removable.

Moore, James Cabinet-maker who from 1714 to 1726 (the year of his death) was in partnership with John Gumley. Moore was presumably proud of his gilt gesso furniture for he incised his name on some pieces (there are examples at Hampton Court). He was employed at Blenheim by the Duchess of Marlborough and supplied furniture to William Kent's designs for Kensington Palace.

Moorfields Carpets The most esteemed of early English carpets, as made by Thomas Moore at Moorfields, London, from about 1760. Loosely knotted (about twenty to the square inch) in the Turkish manner, Moore's carpets were commissioned by Robert Adam (q.v.) and wealthy owners of grand houses of that time. They are very scarce and very expensive.

Mortar A vessel (for use with a pestle) that was made from very early times when they were usually of stone. Bronze was the normal metal used from the Middle Ages. Examples from the sixteenth and seventeenth centuries are quite common; they were not made much after the middle of the eighteenth century.

Mortise and Tenon The mortise is the receptacle, the cavity, which should be an exact fit to take the tenon or tongue. With dovetailing (q.v.) this is the joiner's favoured joint in furniture-making. Dates from the sixteenth century.

Mortise Lock *See* **Locks.**

Mosaic Glass Opaque ware, of dark purple and white swirled appearance. Also known as 'purple marble glass'.

Mother-of-pearl A substance forming the inner layer of some shells. It was probably first used in the East as a decorative inlay. It became popular in Restoration England for the ornament of furniture when it was used in conjunction with bone and ivory. In the second half of the eighteenth century it was used freely on boxes and tea-caddies and in the nineteenth century on trays. It was also used in English Boulle work.

Moulded Pedestal Stem *See* **Silesian Stem.**

Mouldings As separate members, strips of different patterns and shapes used to surround panels, etc.; in the solid, the shaped decoration given to an edge of a cornice, a lid, etc.

Mounts *Furniture.* Metal mounts to protect weak or vulnerable parts of furniture probably had their origin in ancient times but the French furniture-makers, or more correctly the *fondeurs-doreurs*, of the Louis XIV period developed the decorative mount of ormolu. *Ceramics.* Silver-mounted examples of Chinese porcelain are known from the fifteenth century onwards, and from the seventeenth century onwards European pottery was sometimes mounted in silver or pewter. Ormolu mounting for porcelain was introduced during the eighteenth century. As only the finest wares would be considered worth mounting such specimens are expensive as a rule.

Moustiers   An important French faience manufacturing centre from about 1769, at which date the Clérissy factory was founded. Other factories were established in the area later, but none achieved the high standard or success of the Clérissy family. Pictorial painted decoration in monochrome blue is notable.

Movement   The machinery, the 'works', of a clock or watch.

Mudjar Rugs   Brilliantly tinted and often containing as many as ten colours, with characteristic main stripe of border made up of squares round diamonds with roses within, like tessellated tiles. Red selvage. Forty-five to sixty-five knots to square inch.

Muntin   Upright between panels.

Murano   Island near Venice to which the glass-houses of that city were transferred in the thirteenth century owing to the danger of fire. Venetian glass is often called Murano glass.

Murrhine or Murrine   Early mosaic ware from the East which found, in the form of bowls and cups, much favour with the Romans; thought to have been made of precious or semi-precious stones, but perhaps of coloured glass.

Musket   Heavy firearm (14–20 lb.) which probably originated in Spain, whence it was introduced into the Netherlands and then into France and England (by the end of the sixteenth century). Out of favour by 1650, but the term has remained to describe any portable long-arm gun.

Nailsea Glass   Glass-house founded 1788 by John R. Lucas at Nailsea, near Bristol. Several types of glass made: at first bottle-glass of brownish-green tint with flecking or mottling and white enamel decoration, and a light green bottle-glass with crackling or white enamel decoration; then, from *c*. 1815, opaque coloured glass with looped and mottled or flecked decoration, also white and coloured *latticino* in pale green and clear flint glass; from 1845 translucent coloured flint glass. Nailsea produced what is probably the most flamboyant glass ever made in England; the combinations of colours would tax a mathematician; the number and variety of 'friggers' (q.v.) produced must have been phenomenal. Colourful to the last, the Nailsea Glass-house closed in 1873, £30,000 in the red.

Nantgarw This porcelain factory founded in 1813 by William Billingsley who had been at Derby. Billingsley produced porcelain of exceptional translucency, almost like glass. But kiln wastage was so high, sometimes 90 per cent, that the enterprise was bound to fail, and in 1814 the factory was transferred to Swansea (q.v.). Billingsley returned to Nantgarw (1817–20) but was unable to evolve a commercially successful formula. Inevitably Nantgarw porcelain is very scarce. The soft, Sèvres-like paste is highly esteemed by collectors. Some of the wares produced were decorated at Nantgarw but most were

NANT GARW
C.W.   Nantgarw china mark

sent to London for that purpose. The usual mark is 'NANT GARW' in rough capitals with 'c.w.' smaller underneath (probably standing for 'China Works').

Neale, James Pottery manufacturer active at Hanley, 1776–1800, who worked with various partners and traded as Neale & Palmer, Neale & Co., Neale & Wilson; made cream-coloured wares but the best-known products are those in imitation of Wedgwood, jasper, basalts, etc.; this firm's Toby jugs are notable.

Nef Table ornament in the form of a ship.

Neo-classic Of the eighteenth-century classical revival.

Nest of Drawers The case of small drawers, or diminutive chest of drawers, was often so termed in the eighteenth century.

Nest of Tables Graduated tables made to fit one below the other were first made towards the end of the eighteenth century. Four was the normal number and for this reason they were called '*Quartetto*' tables.

Netsuke (Japanese, pronounced 'netsky', from *ne*—a root, and *tsuke*—to fasten) A toggle with holes used to secure the cord on which a man carried his personal belongings. Very old, but as works of art date from late sixteenth to late nineteenth centuries. Tiny, of wood, ivory, bone, horn, amber, often exquisitely carved and fashioned into fantastic human, animal or mythological figures. If made of two materials, then probably of late date.

Nevers Important French centre for the manufacture of faience from the late sixteenth century, the craft having been brought to the district by Italian potters. Several factories flourished in the seventeenth century and for much of the eighteenth and the wares produced are among the best ever made in France. The Chinese influence, not only in decoration but also in shapes, was strong in the last quarter of the seventeenth century.

New Hall The factory founded about 1781 by a group of Staffordshire potters who manufactured hard-paste porcelain to the formula that Richard Champion had used at Bristol and which he had got from Cookworthy. From about 1810 onwards bone-china was made. New Hall porcelain is not so

New Hall china marks

esteemed as Plymouth and Bristol. Early wares are often decorated in the Chinese manner; elaborate painting and gilding is typical. The letter 'N' accompanied by a number was the usual porcelain mark; the name 'New Hall' encircled was applied to bone-china.

Niderviller   French ceramics factory founded about 1754 for the production of faience. Porcelain seems to have been made here from about 1765, though very little, if any, survives from that date. The factory changed hands in 1771 and several times thereafter but it is still in existence. Figures of excellent quality are the most esteemed product of Niderviller.

Nien Hao (Chinese)   Reign mark.

Night Clock   Clock which usually has a pierced dial so that a light placed behind it will enable the time to be seen in the dark.

Night Table   The successor to the close-stool (q.v.). The night table dates from the middle of the eighteenth century, is nearly always on legs, is sometimes combined with a washing stand, frequently has additional drawers and a tray-shaped top and may have a tambour front. Some are like a small chest of drawers.

Nock, Henry   London gunsmith of the eighteenth century. In 1787 he invented a breech plug, 'Nock's Patent Breech', the feature of which was that a thin gold or platinum touch-hole instantly communicated the flash to an antechamber within. (Thus a flintlock with this patent breech cannot be older than 1787.)

Non(e)such   The term is applied to a chest with an inlaid decorative design of architectural representations. These chests were made during the latter half of the sixteenth century, on the Continent and in Germany particularly. The name comes from the palace of Nonsuch at Cheam built by Henry VIII.

Norman, Samuel   Cabinet-maker and carver who did work for Woburn Abbey in the 1750's. He redecorated the picture gallery and the principal drawing-room and supplied furniture including a 'Grand State Bed'.

Nottingham   From *c.* 1690 to 1800 Nottingham was an important pottery centre, being famous for its brown salt-glazed stoneware. The glaze has a strange metallic gleam to it. Decoration is usually incised. Owl and bear jugs (the detachable heads are cups) were a speciality.

Nove   A maiolica factory had been in existence at Nove, Venice, for many years before attempts were made to manufacture soft-paste porcelain about 1752. Porcelain was produced here until about 1835. A star, sometimes with the word 'Nove', is the usual mark.

Nulling   *See* **Gadrooning.**

Nuremberg Egg   Early German watches are so called; the term is a complete misnomer.

Nuremberg Faience   Nuremberg, Bavaria, was an important centre for the manufacture of faience from the sixteenth century. Superbly decorated jugs of the seventeenth century are particularly esteemed. (Nuremberg was celebrated for its *hausmalerei*, i.e. painting done by private decorators working at home.)

Nymphenburg   This hard-paste porcelain factory founded in 1753, with J. J. Ringler from Vienna (q.v.) as arcanist. Situated first at Neudeck, the factory was transferred to premises in the grounds of Nymphenburg Palace in 1761. Under the patronage of Prince Max III Joseph of Bavaria and, more actively, Count Sigismund von Haimhausen, and with the services of one of the greatest European modellers, Franz Anton Bustelli, the factory flourished until about 1770 and then went into a slow decline, passed to the State, was leased to a private company in 1862 and continues in production. Nymphenburg's great reputation is due to the figures of Bustelli, chief modeller from 1754 to 1763. He was the master of the rococo in terms of porcelain, or at least the Bavarian expression of it. The most common Nymphenburg mark is the shield.

Nyon Swiss porcelain factory near Geneva that produced hard-paste porcelain from 1781 till 1813. The mark is a fish in underglaze blue.

Oak A hard and heavy wood, the most common species in England being the common oak and the sessile-fruited oak. Native and imported oak was practically the 'universal timber' for furniture till the Restoration and remained in use in country districts throughout the eighteenth century for 'yeoman' and farmhouse furniture. The 'age of oak' 1100–1660.

Objets d'Art Valuable small items that cannot be classified under other headings.

Oeben, Jean Francois (?–1763) One of the greatest of French cabinet-makers who made much furniture for Louis XV; particularly esteemed are his superbly made bureaux, elaborately fitted with secret drawers and locking devices. Oeben is said to have died a bankrupt (a small marquetry table of his sold at Christie's in 1958 for 34,000 guineas), but his widow continued the business, which thrived when she married his former assistant, Riesener (q.v.).

Ogee (*Cyma Reversa*) A moulding consisting of a double curve, convex above and concave below.

Ogee Bowl A favoured shape for the bowl of drinking glasses in the second half of the eighteenth century. The bowl curves out from the stem, then in a little and then out again—like an elongated S.

Okawachi Japanese porcelain factory near Arita; founded in the mid-seventeenth century; made stoneware and porcelain.

Olivewood A close-grained wood of greenish yellow colour that was used for parquetry, particularly during the late Stuart period.

Omnium A Whatnot (q.v.).

O'Neale, Jeffrey H. Eighteenth-century ceramic artist and miniaturist who worked at Chelsea and later as an outside decorator did a lot of work for the Worcester porcelain factory.

Opaline Semi-translucent milk white glass which glows when held up to light.

Opaque-twist Glass Stems (*See* **Latticino.**) Came into favour about 1745 and stayed there till the end of the century.

Ormolu Bronze, or brass of high purity containing an admixture of zinc, cast in ornamental forms and gilded; the use particularly favoured by the French for furniture mounts, clock-cases, vases, candlesticks, chandeliers. (See next entry.)

Or Moulu A gilt made from a fusion of finely ground gold with mercury, which came to mean the gilded metal itself, 'ormolu'.

Orrery A mechanism representing the motions of the planets round the sun, invented by George Graham, *c.* 1700, and named after Charles, Earl of Orrery, for whom a copy of the invention was made.

Ottoman A backless upholstered sofa in what English cabinet-makers of the late eighteenth and early nineteenth centuries supposed to be the Turkish manner. Usually the ottoman is long and low but sometimes the term is used to describe what is little more than an upholstered stool.

Ouchak Rugs From the great weaving centre of Ouchak in Asia Minor; valuable specimens can be found dating back to the sixteenth century. The earliest have medallion and Turkish scroll designs; 'White' Ouchaks with white or ivory ground date from the seventeenth century. Can be very coarse (sixteen to seventy-two knots) but extremely durable and of carpet size.

Outside Decorators Independent specialists in the decoration of porcelain to whom the factories sent their wares in the 'biscuit' state for painting, enamelling and gilding. Some Outside Decorators purchased the undecorated porcelain; others solicited work.

Over-glaze Decoration applied to pottery and porcelain after glazing.

Overlay Glass *See* **Cased Glass.**

Ovolo A convex moulding of which the section is a quarter-circle. The popular term is 'quarter-round'. Ovolo mouldings with egg-and-dart enrichment was a favoured ornament on furniture in the sixteenth and seventeenth centuries.

Owl Jug Jug in the form of an owl; the detachable head is a cup. Made in earthenware (and stoneware) from as early as the mid-sixteenth century in Germany, and a popular Staffordshire product of the eighteenth century.

Oyster Veneer Veneer made up of discs (cross-sections) of wood cut from branches of trees and laid together as parquetry. Finely grained light-coloured woods were used.

Pagoda The canopied Eastern temple was a favoured decorative motif in the middle of the eighteenth century; cabinet-makers used it a lot.

Pair-case Watch Watch in which the movement is contained in an inner case which in turn fits into an outer, protective case; made from the mid-seventeenth century.

Pai Ting (Chinese) The finest creamy-white Ting ware (q.v.).

Pai Tun Tzu (Chinese) China stone. *See* **Porcelain.**

Pai Tzu (Chinese) White porcelain.

Paktong (Chinese) An alloy of copper, nickel and zinc which, when polished, resembles silver. It stood up well to hard wear and was used for many domestic utensils including grates and fenders in the second half of the eighteenth century. The Chinese seem to have been the first to utilize the metal. Also known as *Tutenag*.

Palissy, Bernard (?1510–89) A famous name in European ceramics; is said to have spent sixteen years perfecting an enamel surface on pottery. He succeeded in 1557 when he began to make the remarkable pieces still to be seen in the Louvre, with plants, shells, animals and insects in relief, and covered with coloured glazes. A Huguenot, he died in the Bastille.

Pallet In an escapement (q.v.), the leaves that actually bed in the teeth of the escape wheel.

Palm Cup Cup without handles.

Palmer, Humphrey Potter of Hanley, active from about 1760, who imitated Wedgwood's basalts, jasper and other wares with considerable success. Towards the end of the 1770's he got into financial difficulties and went into partnership with James Neale (q.v.).

P'an (Chinese) Ancient bronze vessel, a shallow bowl, sometimes with handles.

Panel A surface framed within a larger surface. A panel may be sunk below the framework or raised above it. In construction, the term means a board held in place by a surrounding framework of grooved rails and stiles, the panel fitting into the grooves.

Pap Boat Bowl with a lip for feeding infants; of silver usually; eighteenth-century examples are to be encountered.

Paperweight (Glass) Specimens of *millefiori* (q.v.) glass were shown at a Paris exhibition in 1844 and the following year paperweights were described as 'a new item of trade, the round shaped *millefiori* paperweights of transparent glass in which are inserted quantities of small tubes of all colours and forms to look like a multitude of florets'. The manufacture of these paperweights in France centred at St Louis, Baccarat and Clichy. In England they were produced at the glass-making towns of Bristol, Stourbridge, Birmingham, London, etc. Examples produced after 1865 tend to be inferior in colouring and quality.

Papier Mâché French name (=chewed paper) for an English invention. In 1772 Henry Clay of Birmingham patented his process for making 'paper ware' from linen rags. A cheaper method of making 'papier mâché japan furniture' from rag pulp was patented by Richard Brindley, also of Birmingham, in 1836. Not till the 1860's were both types of furniture known as 'papier mâché'. Clay's ware, handmade, is lighter, perfectly smooth, very tough; Brindley's pressed ware tends to be brittle, and because of this perfect examples are rare. Decoration: the gold is leaf or powder, not paint; pearl shell dates from the 1820's; oil painting from the 30's.

Parcel-gilt Partially gilt.

Parian Ware Unglazed, vitrified porcelain, smooth, like marble (name derives from antique marble found on Paros), made first by Copeland about 1842(?) and later by Minton, and at Belleek. Busts and figures are notable. Really, Parian is an improvement on Derby biscuit porcelain.

Paris Porcelain so designated should have been made at or near Paris. Quite a number of factories were established in the environs of Paris from the 1770's onwards; most of them made hard-paste porcelain. A few of the better-known: *La Courtille*, from about 1770, with porcelain in the German manner the speciality; *Clignancourt*, from 1775, under royal patronage, made Sèvres-like wares; *Rue Popincourt*, from 1782, one of the larger Paris factories, noted for porcelain clock-cases; *Fontainebleau*, from 1795. The main speciality of the Paris factories seems to have been forging the early products of the more famous French factories.

Parquetry Mosaic of wood applied to a ground in simple geometrical forms. It is a form of decorative veneer and was often used with marquetry. Its use in England dates from the second half of the seventeenth century; it was little used in the first half of the eighteenth century but it came back into favour in the last quarter of the eighteenth century. The term also applies to a flooring of small blocks of wood arranged in geometrical patterns.

Partridge Wood Red-brown Brazilian wood used in parquetry, inlay and veneer.

Pâte-de-Verre (French) In the nineteenth century the French successfully revived an old glass-making technique which involved the use of powdered glass of several colours which was mixed and re-fired.

Pâte Dure (French) Hard-paste porcelain.

Paten Small, circular, ecclesiastical plate, usually of silver.

Patera A saucer or dish used for libations or sacrifices by the Greeks and Romans: hence a shallow disc or roundel used as ornament.

Pâte-sur-Pâte (French=clay on clay) Porcelain decoration by means of painting in a white or tinted slip; first used at Sèvres about the middle of the nineteenth century and introduced into England by Marc Solon about 1870 when he left the French factory to come and work at Mintons.

Pâte Tendre (French) Soft-paste porcelain.

Patina (1) *Furniture.* The surface condition that comes about by natural means, rubbing, polishing, usage. (2) *Metal.* The oxidized surface condition of bronzes and other metalwork brought about by natural or artificial means.

Pear Wood Reddish wood with fine grain; used for marquetry and inlaying.

Péché Mortel (French)   A couch that is a glorified upholstered arm-chair and stool. A form of the *Duchesse* (q.v.).

Pedestal   The base of a column in architecture and carried over into furniture in the same sense.

Pedestal Table   The term is applied to two types of table: (1) a circular table on a central pillar terminating in three club or ball-and-claw-footed legs, and (2) a library table with two matching, square pedestals at each end.

Pediment   A triangular structure like a low gable as over a portico in Greek architecture. In furniture, the same structure surmounts the cornices of bookcases, mirrors, cabinets.

Peg Tankard   Silver tankard with a vertical row of pegs or studs inside, these being fitted at regular intervals and intended to measure the amount consumed by communal drinkers. Seventeenth century.

Pembroke Table   A small table with drop-leaf sides supported by brackets, and (usually) a shallow drawer. The name may derive from the Countess of Pembroke; it seems to have been first applied in the 1760's. This piece of furniture, whether as a breakfast table or a lady's work table, was very popular in the late eighteenth century. Both Hepplewhite and Sheraton designed examples.

Pendulum   The incorporation of a pendulum in a clock is attributed to a Dutchman, in 1657, though there is some evidence to suggest that Italian clock-makers had done so earlier. Early bob-pendulums are short and, as used with the verge escapement, swung through an arc of 35 to 40 degrees. With the invention of the anchor escapement about 1670 a much longer pendulum became practicable; known as the Royal pendulum, it was 39·1393 inches long and moved through an arc of 4 or 5 degrees to a one-second beat, thus permitting a second hand and leading to the long-case clock. Early pendulum rods, often of simple iron wire, were liable to expansion and contraction with changes of temperature. Two main improvements, invented about the same time (*c.* 1726), were the mercury pendulum and the grid-iron pendulum. The former, invented by George Graham, had as a bob a glass jar of mercury suspended from a brass pendulum rod; heat that lengthened the rod also expanded the mercury and thus the centre of oscillation remained constant (and *vice versa* in cold weather). The grid-iron pendulum of John Harrison is based on the fact that the expansion of brass to steel is in the ratio of 3 to 2; in his pendulum the upper extremities of alternate brass and steel rods, in the aforementioned ratio as regards length, will therefore if joined at their lower ends remain the same distance apart whatever the changes of temperature. Both the mercury and grid-iron pendulum are still in use today. Very rare is the 'second-and-a-quarter' pendulum in which the duration of each arc of the swing is $1\frac{1}{4}$ seconds and the pendulum is 5 feet in length: introduced *c.* 1675, probably by William Clement, but abandoned by the end of the next decade.

Pergolesi, M. A. Italian who came to Britain in late 1750's and worked for the Adam brothers. His series of *Original Designs* (1777–1800) were behind much of the painted furniture of the period.

Perrott, Humphrey English glass-maker who revolutionized glass manufacture in 1734 by designing a furnace which permitted higher temperatures, greater blast, larger melting pots.

Petronel A large pistol with a stock; sixteenth century.

Petuntse China stone. *See* **Porcelain.**

Pewter An alloy of tin with an admixture of another metal—usually lead, but sometimes brass or copper. This alloy can be worked by casting, also by turning and hammering. The Romans made pewter of high quality and design. In medieval times the tableware of kings and the nobility was of pewter. In England the Pewterers' Guild was officially recognized in 1348; by the end of the fifteenth century pewter had almost superseded treen (wooden platters); in 1504 marking was made compulsory (the rule much flouted, of course), standards of 'London quality' were set. There was much pewter produced in France, Germany and Switzerland from the fourteenth century onwards; the English product is plain compared to most Continental pewter. Though earthenware came into common use in the seventeenth century, pewter held its own till almost the end of the eighteenth century; but Britannia metal (q.v.) killed the art, which, by 1850, was almost extinct, though certain articles such as tankards and measures continued (and continue) to be made.

Pharmacy Jars The blue and white jars bearing the names of drugs date from the middle of the seventeenth century; squat tin-enamelled jars are usually earlier.

Pianoforte A keyboard instrument in which the strings are struck, not plucked. The piano was invented by Bartolomeo Cristofori of Florence in the early years of the eighteenth century. The first English piano was made about 1760: it was small and rectangular and, as regards shape, looked to the virginal and clavichord (qq.v.). This type of piano, four to five feet long, was called the 'square' piano and was made in considerable numbers for the remainder of the eighteenth century. The 'upright' piano came into favour about 1800, but meantime the 'grand', based on the harpsichord shape, had evolved in the 1780's.

Pie Crust Table Round-topped table on a tripod base, the dish-top (q.v.) having a scalloped edge. Made from the mid-eighteenth century onwards.

Pied de Biche Hoof-foot.

Pien Yao (Chinese) Ceramics with *flambé* glaze (q.v.).

Pierced Ware Pottery in which the decoration is pierced right through the ware, a speciality at Leeds (q.v.) from the 1760's, but practised at many Staffordshire potteries too. The inspiration derives from such decoration on silver.

Pier Glass A mirror made to hang in the wall space between windows. Usually in pairs, they were tall and narrow, the frames often gilded and carved. They date from the beginning of the eighteenth century.

Pier Table A table meant to stand against the wall between windows. Many are D-shaped. The pier table is a form of side-table which, like the pier glass (*see* last entry), dates from the beginning of the eighteenth century.

Pilaster A rectangular pillar engaged in a wall and projecting only a fraction of its breadth. Carried over from architecture to furniture, pilasters are employed at corners of bureaux, cabinets, etc., also to divide fronts and frame doors.

Pinchbeck An alloy (comprising chiefly zinc and copper) of a gold colour invented by the London clock-maker Christopher Pinchbeck, 'the only Maker of the True and genuine metal' which, it was claimed, was not to be distinguished by the nicest eye from real gold. It was used for many small items in the eighteenth century.

Pinewood Timber from a genus of resin-producing trees, having a straight grain and being easy to work. Little used before the Restoration, it was employed for carcase work in veneer furniture and for such carved and gilt furniture as picture frames and cabinet-stands. During the eighteenth century it was used a good deal for carvers' pieces.

Pinxton A small porcelain factory was established at Pinxton, Derbyshire, by William Billingsley in 1796, perhaps in partnership with John Coke, on whose estate the factory was situated. Coke almost certainly provided the capital to launch the

Pinxton china marks

enterprise. Billingsley pulled out in 1801 but the factory continued in being till about 1812, latterly under the management,
perhaps ownership, of John Cutts, a painter responsible for
much of the decoration.

Most of the porcelain produced, mainly table wares and
small vases, was in the style of Derby; but after Billingsley left
there was a considerable deterioration. Output was always
small and Pinxton porcelain is accordingly scarce. A large-
headed arrow is a recurring mark.

Pipe Rack Various types for holding clay pipes include
(1) metal frame for cleaning pipes on a hot oven—also known
as a pipe-kiln; (2) wooden stand fitted with a pierced disc, on
a central standard, through which the stems of the pipes
passed; (3) a hanging rack of wood constructed to hold pipes
in a horizontal position supported on indented uprights;
(4) a wooden fixture with a backboard fitted with two narrow
cross bars pierced to receive the pipes.

Planewood Timber of the maple-leaved plane which, according to the *Cabinet Dictionary* (1803), was used instead of beech
by country furniture-makers for painted chairs.

Plaque An ornamental plate affixed to furniture, chimney-
pieces, etc. Wedgwood plaques are notable; metal, chiefly
bronze, plaques for the decoration of furniture were favoured
during the Regency.

Plaquette A small plaque (like a medal) for the decoration of
furniture and domestic utensils.

Plate Wares of gold, solid silver or silver-gilt. Because of
possible (and frequent) confusion the terms 'gold plate' and
'silver plate' are often used; this is particularly the case with the
latter in order to distinguish such wares from Sheffield plate,
electro-plate, etc.

Plateau A stand resting on a plinth or short legs, serving as a
centre ornament for the dining-table. In fashion during the late
years of the eighteenth century and early in the nineteenth

century. Some are in fact a mirror in a metal frame and may have a low decorative gallery.

Plate Money The largest coins ever made, square-shaped, being sometimes 40 lb. in weight (the copper equivalent of what was the silver value); a Swedish curiosity issued in the seventeenth and eighteenth centuries.

Plate Pail A bucket or basket-like container for carrying plates from the kitchen to the dining-room; used in big houses during the eighteenth century when such a journey could be an arduous one. Nearly always of mahogany, the shape was usually circular or polygonal, there would be an open section for easy access, and the handle was most often of brass.

Plinth In architecture, the square base of a column, and by analogy the base of a piece of furniture, etc., when not supported on feet.

Plique â Jour *See* **Enamel.**

Plumwood Yellow wood with red heart, very hard, used in country furniture.

Plymouth The first hard-paste porcelain to be made in England was made at Coxside, Plymouth, by William Cookworthy, who patented his formula and founded the Plymouth factory in 1768. But in 1770 the factory, which seems to have been financially unsound from the start, was moved to Bristol, and in 1773 Cookworthy withdrew from the venture.

Plymouth china marks

Inevitably Plymouth porcelain is scarce. The body is very hard. Clumsiness of execution and decoration is typical, with frequent smoke stains, firecracks, specks and warping and running. Decoration includes underglaze blue (which looks greyish), enamel painting, and things like salt cellars and sauce boats are often ornamented in relief with shells, coral and seaweed, but much Plymouth porcelain is undecorated.

And much Plymouth porcelain is unmarked. A few pieces bear the complete name PLYMOUTH, and the inscription 'Mr. W. Cookworthy's Factory Plymouth 1770' has been recorded. But many marks were used and continued to be used after the factory was removed to Bristol. Characteristic is the '2/4' mark, the vertical stroke of the four being shaped like a two.

Pole Screen Small screen, often oval in shape, mounted on a tall pole which usually stands on a tripod base. These screens are adjustable, and the panel is frequently of needlework.

Polish (Furniture) The use of oil, linseed particularly, to preserve furniture is of considerable antiquity. From the twelfth to the sixteenth century it was the usual practice to paint furniture. Polishing with oil, turpentine, beeswax, was practised from the sixteenth century. Walnut for use in furniture was sometimes heated and made to 'sweat' and then polished with its own oil. 'French' polish was introduced into England from France about 1820 and much old furniture was scraped and French polished in the nineteenth century.

Polonaise Carpets Persian but with Western influence suggested by the balanced composition and foreign motifs (these superb carpets are something of a puzzle to the experts). Woven of wool but more frequently of silk, and incorporating gold and silver thread, many shades of many colours are exquisitely blended, the larger areas of lighter tones contrasting with small pockets of vivid deep colouring.

Pontil Mark *See* **Punty Mark.**

Pontypool Japanned Ware Local (Pontypool, Monmouthshire) metal ware japanned with a by-product of coal developed by the Allgood family from the latter half of the seventeenth century. Small things such as trays and dressing boxes are typical.

Poplar A timber ranging in colour from whitish yellow to grey; used for inlay in the sixteenth and early seventeenth century.

Porcelain (1) HARD-PASTE. Hard or 'True' porcelain contains two essential ingredients known to the Chinese as *kao-lin* (china clay) and *pai-tun-tzu* (china stone), both of which are products of feldspar rock in varying stages of decay. The main characteristic of *kaolin* is that it will take and retain almost any shape. *Pai-tun-tzu*, or *petuntse*, which is the more usual French form, acts as the cement. *Kaolin* requires a higher temperature to fuse it than does the *petuntse*. The mixture of refractory white *kaolin* and fusible *petuntse* unite in the firing into a dense, white, translucent, resonant material, namely porcelain. The temperature required to bring this about is approximately 1,450 degrees Centigrade. The mixture before firing is usually called the 'paste'.

Porcelain comprises the 'body' and the 'glaze'. The latter is an outer skin containing *petuntse* and in hard porcelain is nearly always fired at the same time as and in one operation with the body. Rarely, the glaze is applied later in a second firing which will be at a somewhat lower temperature. Hard porcelain is translucent though the degree of translucency may vary greatly. It should also 'ring' when struck. And it should be so hard that it will withstand efforts to cut it with the edge of a file. Worth bearing in mind is that for the Chinese the criterion for porcelain is that it 'rings' when struck, whereas for the European translucency is all important.

It is generally agreed that porcelain was first made by the Chinese in the late seventh or early eighth century A.D. A merchant writing in 851 tells of drinking vessels made of a clay as fine as glass through which the shimmer of water could be seen. The body of surviving specimens cannot be scratched with steel and is white and translucent; but it is said that *kaolin* was not used. Those Chinese porcelains with which we are most familiar—of the Ming and Ching dynasties—do contain *kaolin* and a greater proportion of *petuntse* than is usual in European porcelain. This means that the wares are somewhat softer and did not require such a high firing temperature as the European.

The Chinese kept their secret and their monopoly for a millenium and it was not till the early years of the eighteenth century that Johann Friedrich Böttger produced the first true porcelain to be made in Europe, which led to the founding, in 1710, of the Royal Saxon Porcelain Manufacture at Meissen, near Dresden. A factory was established at Vienna some ten years later and by the mid-eighteenth century there were a number of German factories producing hard porcelain. Sèvres, which at first had made soft-paste porcelain, introduced a hard-paste body in 1770. It may be said that on the Continent soft-paste formulae were used only until such time as the hard-paste formula could be obtained.

But this was not so in England, where true porcelain has been but little made. William Cookworthy experimented for many years before founding his factory at Plymouth in 1768. He made hard-paste porcelain there till 1770 when the factory was removed to Bristol. Cookworthy soon withdrew from the enterprise which continued under Richard Champion till about 1782. Some hard-paste porcelain was made at the small New Hall (Staffordshire) factory from about 1780 to 1812. All the other English factories made soft-paste porcelains. But from the early years of the nineteenth century 'bone china' was the staple English product.

Porcelain (2) SOFT-PASTE. Soft or 'artificial' porcelain differs from hard-paste porcelain (*see* above) in that it is a 'softer' material, that it requires less heat (about 1,100 degrees Centigrade as against 1,450 degrees Centigrade for hard) to fuse it, that it can be scratched or cut with metal (the edge of a file) that the glaze was always added afterwards.

It was inevitable the European potters desirous of producing a ware that would partake of the translucency of Chinese porcelain should introduce glass into the mix. This was first done successfully at Florence about 1560, the product being known as Medici porcelain. Surviving examples are very rare indeed. It was not till the beginning of the eighteenth century that any great quantity of porcelain was produced. St Cloud was probably the first successful French factory (from before 1700), followed by Chantilly, Mennecy, Vincennes, Sèvres; in Italy, Nove (before 1730), Doccia, Capo-di-Monte . . .

Whereas in Europe the basic ingredients were clay and ground glass, in England bone-ash and, in a few cases, soaprock, were preferred to glass. Bone-ash makes for easier working and seems to have been first used at Bow about 1750, then later at Chelsea, Derby and other centres. Soaprock was first used at Bristol in 1748, other factories to use it being Worcester, Caughley, Liverpool.

Porringer   A deep bowl with upright sides and an almost flat bottom and two handles or ears. Unlike the posset-pot (q.v.) the porringer rarely has a cover and was intended for porridge

A silver porringer, 1706

and broth rather than hot drinks. The so-called bleeding-bowls were probably small porringers before imagination got to work on them.

Porter's Chair   Chair for use of servant on duty in the halls of large houses; upholstered in leather and with enclosed (arched) top to keep out draughts.

Portland Vase   A vase of cameo glass thought to have been made at Alexandria about the time of Christ. Its various owners included the Duchess of Portland; hence the name. The vase was lent to the British Museum and was smashed by an idiot in 1845 (it has been restored). But before this tragedy took place Wedgwood had made a copy of the vase in his jasper ware (q.v.), a task that took him three years, 1786–90. A number of specimens were made and there have been subsequent editions.

Posset-pot A caudle cup, forerunner of the porringer, dating from the seventeenth century. The form is usually bell-shaped and nearly all posset-pots have (or had) a cover. Silver examples are the most esteemed, naturally, but they are very scarce and the collector is more likely to encounter specimens of pottery. *See* **Porringer.**

Potato Ring Circular silver stand, probably for a bowl or dish, usually embossed and/or pierced; made in Ireland in the second half of the eighteenth century.

Pot Board Low shelf under a dresser.

Pot Bracket A pivoting iron bracket, from which pots could be suspended, that swings out over the fire.

Pot Crane A pot bracket (*see* above) with a crane-like device for lowering or raising the pot(s).

Pothanger or Hake or Hook The hook that hung from pot bracket and crane, sometimes with a ratchet for adjusting height.

Pot Lids The lids of jars made to contain pomades, etc. Decoration is polychrome colour printing under the glaze done by a mechanical process. Nineteenth century.

Pottery Generic term applied to all ceramic substances other than porcelain (though, all too often, porcelain is included under this heading); the two types of pottery are earthenware and stoneware (qq.v.). Pottery is simply clay baked to a certain degree of hardness which will vary according to the duration and intensity of the firing. Such elements as sand or calcined flints are added to certain wares.

Pounce   The powder formerly used to dry ink was so-called. The pounce-box or pounce-pot was the container-cum-sprinkler. By extension a fine 'powdered' (matted) effect on metal was termed 'pouncing'.

Powder Blue   Ceramic decoration, under the glaze, in which the powdered pigment is blown on the ware; first used by the Chinese in the second half of the seventeenth century and later copied by many European factories (notably Worcester in England).

Pratt Ware   Earthenware decorated with high-temperature colours as made by Felix Pratt of Lane Delph. Robust jugs, often with decoration in relief, bearded faces, and figures, are quite common. The Pratt family were active throughout the nineteenth century.

Press Bed   A folding bed made to pack into a concealing press or cupboard.

Pressed Glass   Glass made in a mould without blowing. The mould is partly filled with molten glass and a plunger, conforming to the inside shape of the vessel being made, is thrust into the mould and presses the molten glass into the cavities of the mould. First made in the United States about 1827, the invention usually credited to Enoch Robinson, and soon taken up in England.

Pricket   A spike for holding a candle, used in candlesticks before the introduction of the socket or nozzle. The term seems also to have been applied to the candle itself.

Prie-Dieu (French = pray God)   Kneeling desk, usually of oak, the hinged kneeling step a box for devotional books. Also *prie-dieu chair*: low seat and tall straight back with flat top on which the arms rest when praying.

Princewood   Kingwood (q.v.).

Privy Council Ware *See* **Shu Fu.**

Prunt Small piece of ornamental glass, often shaped or impressed to represent blackberry or raspberry, dropped or laid on to a vase or other vessel.

Prunus Vase *See* **Mei Ping.**

Punch Bowl Silver punch bowls began to be made after the Restoration; the earliest examples are quite shallow; those dating from the end of the seventeenth century are larger and usually have removable rims or 'collars' (*see* **Monteith**). Large bowls of pottery and porcelain were made by English factories in the eighteenth century, and these also formed a profitable branch of the Chinese export trade.

Punch Glass Made from *c.* 1690. The bowl should be plain, clear, unadorned. Hot punch became popular about 1763 and punch glasses with handles were made from that time.

Punty Mark The mark or scar under old blown glass made by the punty rod, with which the glass was held after removal from the blowpipe. 'Punty' is sometimes spelt 'pontil'.

Purdonium Square wooden box with hinged lid, padded seat, removable container, for storing coal at fireside; often in pairs; Victorian.

Puzzle Jug Pottery drinking jug, usually with a full, pierced neck, which contains a hidden tube that enables the contents to be drained by suction. Several apertures (including one that may be hidden) are available to the drinker; he must drink from one, which he can only do if he successfully blocks all the others. Made at various centres during the seventeenth and eighteenth centuries; humorous inscriptions are often found on these jugs.

Quaich (Scottish) A shallow, circular drinking vessel, like a deep saucer, with two (occasionally three) lugs or flat handles.

Quare, Daniel (?1651–1724) Notable London clock-maker who made every kind of clock and whose workmanship ranged from the superb to the ordinary; invented the repeating watch; also made many barometers. A man of great versatility and industry, Quare is esteemed for the quality of his best clocks and for his Quaker integrity.

Quarrel or Quarry Pane of glass as used for glazing lattice windows.

Quartetto Tables *See* **Nest of Tables.**

Quatrefoil Decorative motif formed of four leaves set at right angles to one another within a circle.

Queen's Ware The name Wedgwood (q.v.) gave to his creamware (q.v.).

Rabbet A recess made along the edge of a piece of timber to allow lodgment for another piece. Sometimes spelt *rebate*.

Rack and Snail Striking Horological term for the system of striking the hours and the quarters invented by Edward Barlow in 1676 and first used by Tompion. It was this system of striking that made repeating clocks possible. One advantage is that the hour hand can be moved round without pausing at every revolution to allow the striking sequence to strike as the 'snail' (a cam-shaped disc) moves with the hour wheel.

Rail Constructional member in a horizontal position.

Ratafia Glass Name given to a cordial glass of flute form popular in the second half of the eighteenth century. Ratafia was a brandy flavoured with fruit cordials.

Ravenscroft, George (1618–81) English glass-maker, made flint glass 1674; improved on it with his 'glass of lead' 1675.

Rebate *See* **Rabbet.**

Red Ware   Red stoneware as made by the Elers (q.v.), Astbury (q.v.) and other Staffordshire potters from the late seventeenth century to the end of the eighteenth. Wedgwood called his improved red ware *Rosso Antico*.

Reeding   Ornament comprising a group of two (or more) beads in parallel lines.

Refectory Table   Term for a long table such as might have been used in the refectory of monasteries but applied to long oak tables from the halls of domestic buildings.

Reform Flasks   Salt-glazed stoneware flasks made in the form of political figures at the time of the Reform Bill (1832).

Régence   French period of the Regency of the Duke of Orleans, 1715–23, a period of transition, stylistically speaking, from Louis XIV to Louis XV, from the baroque to the rococo.

Regency   Strictly, the period 1811–20; but an extension has been allowed and the period 1800–37 is generally understood and accepted.

Regulator   A precision, long-case clock, usually made for scientific purposes.

Rent Table   Circular or polygonal-topped table with drawers in the frieze. First made in the middle of the eighteenth century and popular well into the nineteenth. Also called *Drum* or *Capstan* table.

Repeater   Clock or watch with a 'pull-repeating' mechanism by means of which the hours and quarters can be struck at will by pulling a cord.

Repoussé (French)   Relief decoration on metal by hammering the reverse side.

Reredo   *See* **Fire-back.**

Resist Overglaze ceramic decoration making use of silver or other metallic lustre, the pattern being painted upon the glaze with a substance that 'resists' the pigment then applied. *See* **Lustre.**

Revere, Paul (1735–1818)   Born in Boston, U.S.A., son of a French silversmith who had emigrated to America. The third of twelve children, Paul took over his father's business on the latter's death in 1754 and became the greatest American silversmith of his day. (Earned a different reputation for the part he played in the Boston Tea Party and by the famous ride celebrated by Longfellow.)

Ridgway Staffordshire family—the brothers Job and George, and Job's two sons John and William—who made much pottery and porcelain, particularly at the Cauldron Place Works, Shelton, and the Bell Bank Works, Hanley, from the beginning of the nineteenth century.

Riesener, Jean Henri (1734–1806)   One of the greatest of French cabinet-makers; worked in Oeben's (q.v.) workshop, of which he took over the management on Oeben's death and subsequently married the widow; probably made more furniture for the Crown than any other maker. He was much more successful financially than Oeben. Marquetry was his speciality, but he made every type of furniture then in vogue.

Rifling Arquebuses were produced with grooved bores as early as 1460; rifled weapons of high quality were being made throughout Europe by 1525, thus doubling range and accuracy.

Rocaille (French)   A form of decoration based on small rock and shell shapes, whence comes the term *rococo* (q.v.).

Rockingham Pottery was made at the Rockingham Works, Swinton, Yorkshire, from the mid-1740's, the names of Edward Butler, William Malpas, Thomas Bingley and others being associated with these early ventures. In 1806 the Bramelds, trading as Brameld & Co., took over and made earthenware till about 1820 and then bone-porcelain until 1842. Rockingham bone-china comprised a clear white paste with a good

Rockingham china mark

glaze, often decorated lavishly with gilding. Highly decorative table-services were a speciality. The name 'Brameld', sometimes impressed, is a common mark, as is the griffin, from the crest of Earl Fitzwilliam, Marquis of Rockingham.

Rococo A style in art that evolved on and replaced the baroque (q.v.); it had its beginnings in the 1720's, in France, and on its introduction into England in the middle years of the eighteenth century it was known as 'the French taste'. As decoration the style found expression in asymmetrical ornament, favouring shell, rock and floral forms. Thus most of the English porcelain factories produced rococo wares; much English silver of the period is in the rococo style (e.g. Paul de Lamerie); and furniture designs in the rococo style were published by Chippendale, Matthias Lock, Thomas Johnson, Ince and Mayhew. As distinct from baroque, the rococo emphasizes ornament at the expense of form. The severe judgement of Fowler states 'that rococo is regarded as a form taken by baroque when it aimed no longer at astounding the spectator with the marvellous, but rather at amusing him with the ingenious'. The vogue for the rococo lasted till the classical revival of the 1770's.

Roentgen, David (1743–1807) One of the most celebrated of French cabinet-makers, his marquetry pieces being particularly esteemed. He worked not only in France but also in Germany, Italy, Russia.

Roman Striking A power-saving system of clock striking, probably introduced by Joseph Knibb about 1685, which made use of two bells, a smaller and a larger, the former striking I, II, III, the latter striking V and twice for X. In this system only 30 blows in all are needed as against the normal 78 in the run of 12 hours.

Romayne Work Medallions of heads; derived from Italian Renaissance forms.

Römer A German drinking glass first made in the fifteenth century and still being made today. The glass may be tall or stubby, but in most examples the brim will be narrower than the widest swell of the bowl and the stem is usually studded with prunts or small knops, and 'threading' is usual where the bowl meets the stem, which is frequently hollow.

Rose du Barry *See* **Rose Pompadour.**

Rose, John Founder of the Coalport porcelain factory (q.v.).

Rose Maling Painting on peasant furniture, Norwegian, characterized by rose motif, also human and military figures, buildings, acanthus leaves.

Rose Pompadour Rose pink ground colour first used on porcelain at Sèvres about 1757. Also called (incorrectly) *rose du Barry.*

Rosewood Name given to several distinct types of ornamental timber of dark blackish-brown colour, finely marked, which is chiefly used in veneering. The wood was known in the late seventeenth century, used sparingly in the middle years of the eighteenth century, but much favoured during the Regency period.

Rossi Antico The name Josiah Wedgwood gave to his red stoneware.

Roubiliac, Louis Francoise French sculptor who worked in England from 1720 till his death in 1762. He may have been connected with the Chelsea Porcelain Factory.

Rouen Important French centre of the faience industry. Italian potters settled here in the sixteenth century, but the truly French product was made from *c.* 1650 when Edme Poterat established a factory. The fame and popularity of Rouen wares lasted until the end of the eighteenth century. (Experiments in the making of soft-paste porcelain were carried out at Rouen as early as 1673.)

Roundabout Chair Type of armchair, usually of mahogany or walnut, with the legs arranged one at front, one at each side and one at rear, thus enabling the chair to be placed in a corner. Made from early in the eighteenth century. Also known as *Corner Chairs, Writing Chairs.*

Roundel A decorative medallion; bull's-eye glass or bottle glass in early windows and door lights.

Rummer Name given to several types of English drinking glasses: the English version of the *römer* (q.v.); a larger-bowled Georgian goblet; the toddy-rummer (q.v.).

Runner Piece of wood on either side under drawers to support the latter. Also another name for lopers on which the drop-fronts of bureaux are supported.

Sadler & Green Partners in a Liverpool business that specialized in the decoration of pottery (and perhaps manufactured some wares). John Sadler may have been the first to use transfer-printing as a means of decorating ceramics; he is said to have invented the process in 1750. The firm was active throughout the second half of the eighteenth century. Many Staffordshire potters (including Wedgwood) sent large quantities of earthenware to Sadler & Green to be decorated.

Sad Ware Flat articles of pewter.

Saint Cloud Soft-paste porcelain made at this French factory (founded for the production of faience *c.* 1670) from about 1700. Saint Cloud is thus the first French porcelain manufactory. The porcelain was of good quality, slightly yellowish, the decoration at first following that encountered on Rouen faience, and then, from about 1730, the Kakiemon (q.v.) style. The factory closed about 1770. The most common mark is a sun.

Saint Petersburg The Russian Imperial Porcelain Factory was at St Petersburg, Moscow. Porcelain is said to have been manufactured as early as 1744 but little is known of wares produced before 1762. After this date the French style predominates.

Salopian Mark on, and name sometimes given to, Caughley porcelain (q.v.).

Salt Cellar The important position of the great salt cellar on the dining-table in the Middle Ages and during the Renaissance period accounts for the elaborate workmanship bestowed on it. Existing examples of the hour-glass form date from between 1490 and 1525. Then came a different form, either square or circular in plan, the cover raised on brackets, and often surmounted by a figure. The salts known as 'bell salts' which, as the name suggests, expand towards the base, appeared towards the close of the sixteenth century. Small open salts, 'trencher salts', date from the reign of Charles II, when the ceremonial use of the great salt had died out. These small salts, usually bowl-shaped, though box-shaped examples with hinged lids are to be found, remained solid till mid-Georgian times, when pierced work, and glass liners, came into favour.

Salt-glaze Glaze for stoneware (q.v.). Salt is thrown into the kiln when the maximum temperature is reached and the great heat reduces the salt to its component parts, one of which, sodium, combines with silica in the ware to form a thin skin or glaze.

Saltire Stretchers of tables and chairs which cross in X-form, usually with a finial at the crossing.

Samarkand Rugs Rugs that belong in the Chinese group, though the Persian influence is to be detected. Colouring is usually extremely rich. Over-all floral patterns are characteristic; squarish medallions are another favoured motif. Loosely woven with (usually) the Senna knot.

Samson Porcelain Porcelain made from 1845 onwards by Edmé Samson et Cie of Paris who specialized in reproducing old porcelain of many kinds, Chinese armorial porcelain, Meissen figures and the products of Sèvres, Chelsea and Derby. Samson often reproduced the marks too, but, sportingly, frequently included a disguised 's'.

Sand-box Pot, usually of silver or pewter, with perforated lid and containing fine sand for drying ink.

San Tsai (Chinese) 'Three-colour' decoration on Ming stoneware and porcelain; the alkali silicate glazes, coloured with metallic oxides and applied direct to the previously fired body, are kept apart by ridges or engraved lines. Colours used include blue, yellow, turquoise, green.

Sarabend Rugs Persian rugs of fine weave using the Senna knot, the ground—of white, blue or red—being covered with small conical devices set close together; five to seven stripe border.

Sar(o)uk Carpets Persian rugs of fine weave with Senna knot, the medallion a favoured motif, dark blue and red the primary colours; three to seven stripe border; similar to Kashans (q.v.).

Satinwood A number of woods are so called but only two varieties have been much used by English cabinet-makers. One is from the West Indies and the other from the East Indies. Both are yellowish in tone and vary from a plain grain to a mottled figure. The West Indian variety was used as a veneer from the 1760's onwards, and also, but to a lesser extent, in the solid. The East Indian variety was introduced in the late eighteenth century and was similarly employed, and also used for cross-banding. The 'age of satinwood' 1770–1830.

Satsuma Ware Japanese pottery made at Satsuma, on the island of Kyushu, since the early seventeenth century. Many kinds of wares were made, but the cream-coloured pottery decorated with enamel colours and gilding dates from the late eighteenth century.

Savonnerie Carpets These French carpets (so-called because they were first produced in an old soap factory) were made from the second quarter of the seventeenth century. The Turkish knot was used and they have a close-cut pile. Eighteenth century examples are sometimes to be found but at a very high price.

Scagliola (Italian) A composition composed of ground plaster of paris mixed with a solution of glue and coloured to imitate marble. The technique is very old, so that the work of the Italian master mason Guido del Conte (1584–1649), whose scagliola was greatly esteemed, was in the nature of a revival. Slabs of scagliola were much imported into England in the eighteenth century for use as tops of tables and commodes.

Sceaux Faience and porcelain factory founded about 1749 by an architect named de Bey at Sceaux, near Paris. Extremely little porcelain was made until 1775 when the Duc de Penthièvre, High Admiral of France, became patron. Painted decoration is of a high order. The factory closed in 1794. The mark of an anchor is to be encountered.

Sconce Term applied to a wall-light consisting of a candle branch or branches (or tray) and back-plate. The back-plate, which could be of metal or mirror-glass, served as a reflector. Decoration is frequently rich on mid-eighteenth-century examples.

Screen There are three basic types: (1) the folding screen which is made up of leaves hinged (or otherwise connected) and covered with paper, lacquered wood or textiles; (2) a frame standing on a base and feet—i.e. cheval screen; (3) a frame supported on a standard or pole—i.e. pole-screen. The three types were made in considerable quantities during the eighteenth and nineteenth centuries.

Screw-barrel Pistol The barrel screws on to a short breech chamber and is unscrewed for loading. Invented about 1635.

Screws Metal screws for furniture were first used in England towards the end of the seventeenth century. They had a slotted head and the thread was hand-filed. Screws were first produced on a lathe about 1760. The modern machine-made pointed screw came into use in the middle of the nineteenth century.

Scriptor *See* **Scrutoire.**

Scrutoire Form of French *escritoire* or writing cabinet. The term was used in the late seventeenth century for the forerunner of the bureau writing cabinet that came in at the end of the century. A 'scriptor' is the same thing.

'Secret' Decoration *See* **An Hua.**

Seddon, George (1727–1801) Cabinet-maker and successful business man whose mass production methods enabled him to cater for the less than rich; transformed his Aldersgate Street (London) workshops into a forerunner of the modern furnishing store with, by 1786, some 400 employees. His firm flourished well into the nineteenth century.

Senna Rugs Persian rugs of fine texture and short wool pile; over-all decoration of repeated leaf, floral or cone motifs are typical; blue, red or ivory are basic colours, supported by greens, yellows; three-stripe border; Senna knot.

Serpentine Front An undulating front in which the centre is usually convex and the two ends concave. In the case of furniture dating from the middle years of the eighteenth century this shaping was used to display advantageously the figure of veneers. A serpentine-shaping was also freely used for the friezes of tables and rails of seat furniture.

Seto A Japanese ceramics-making centre for many centuries. In the nineteenth century it was at Seto that most of those enormous vases, three feet or more high, were made for export to Europe.

Settee   The term seems to have been first used in England in the early years of the eighteenth century, the word probably being a diminutive of 'settle' (*see* next entry). Many kinds of seat have been described as settees so that the only safe definition is 'a seat with back and arms for two or more persons'. It is difficult to distinguish between a settee and a sofa, but generally a sofa is larger, long enough to allow a person to recline at full length. A particular form of settee that dates from the end of the seventeenth century is the double or treble-chair type. The 'love seat' is a settee—for two only. The 'hall settee' lacks any upholstery or padding and is usually severe; such pieces were specifically designed for the hall during the eighteenth century.

Settle   A long seat (accommodating two or more persons), having a back and arms and an enclosed base; the seat is usually a lid. The settle evolved from the chest, which is what early examples are—plus back and arms. The settle dates back to the fifteenth century, perhaps earlier.

Sèvres   This French porcelain factory founded at Vincennes in 1738 by M. Orry de Fulvi with the help of two workmen from Chantilly. The venture was far from successful and in 1745 a company was formed under the direction of Charles Adam who obtained a thirty-year monopoly from Louis XV and the services of outstanding administrators and workmen. In 1756 the factory was removed to Sèvres where it continues working to this day. Soft-paste porcelain was made until 1769, when a hard paste was introduced, the two being made concurrently, the hard paste slowly ousting the soft. The hard-paste porcelain was termed *Porcelaine Royale* to distinguish it from the soft-paste *Porcelaine de France*, and the former was marked with a crown surmounting the crossed 'L's'.
  Thanks to royal patronage (and its concomitant, severe restrictions imposed on rival ventures) the soft-paste porcelain made at Sèvres from 1756 to 1786 is finer than anything else

The settee. 1, Transitional settle-settee, *c.* 1670. 2, Queen Anne. 3, 2-chair back settee, *c.* 1735. 4, Hepplewhite settee, *c.* 1780

of that period. The famous biscuit porcelain, so suitable for figures and statuettes, was introduced as early as 1751. Painted decoration on coloured ground was superb. Such ground colours as the dark mottled blue (*gros bleu*), turquoise (*bleu celeste*), strong rich blue (*bleu de Roi*), and pink (*rose Pompadour*) were of a richness never achieved before.

Sèvres china marks

Sèvres porcelain of the eighteenth century was made for the wealthy, and the collector who collects it today will have to pay dearly for his predilection. Inevitably it has been faked a lot. The mark is the famous crossed double 'L'.

Sgraffiato or Sgraffito (Italian=scratched) Pottery decoration sometimes used when the slip and the body are of contrasting colours, the design being incised through the slip to reveal the body colour.

Shagreen A term used for (1) the skin of sharks—and other fish—prepared as a covering for boxes, knife-cases, etc., and (2) unstained leather in which a granular surface was obtained by pressing seeds into the material while soft and flexible, this leather when dyed and dried also being used for box and case coverings.

Shaker Furniture The term is used loosely to indicate early American cottage furniture, some of which, no doubt, was made by 'Shakers' (members of a religious sect).

Sham-dram Cheap drinking glass with deceptive bowl that holds less than a publican's measure of Scotch today; humble relation of the toast-master glass (q.v.), made for the use of the tavern-keeper.

Shearer, Thomas Cabinet-maker and designer, a contemporary of Hepplewhite and Sheraton, to whom is often given the credit for first producing what we today think of as the modern sideboard. His designs first appeared in 1788 in *The Cabinet Maker's London Book of Prices*, which was really a trade catalogue, and were re-issued in the same year as *Designs for Household Furniture*.

Sheffield Plate Wares made of copper plated with silver, the sheets of copper being sandwiched by rolling between films of silver. The process was invented by Thomas Bolsover, a Sheffield cutler, in about 1742, but he seems to have made little but buttons with his new ware. The first domestic items, such as coffee pots and candlesticks, were made in the middle 1750's. Matthew Boulton, the Birmingham manufacturer who made the finest English ormolu, was the first to exploit the new process in a big way; he set up a factory for this purpose in 1762. The mid-nineteenth-century invention of electro-plating superseded the making of Sheffield plate.

Sheraton, Thomas (1751–1806) Author and furniture designer who, though trained as a cabinet-maker, was never in business as a manufacturer of furniture. He was born in Stockton-on-Tees, County Durham, and must have come to London before 1791 as in that year the first part of *The Cabinet-Maker's and Upholsterer's Drawing Book* was published. The work was in four parts and came out 1791–4. In 1803 he published the *Cabinet Dictionary*, an illustrated work which not only defined and explained terms used in the trade but also contained directions for varnishing, polishing and gilding. His last work, *The Cabinet-Maker, Upholsterer, and General Artist's Encyclopaedia*, a rambling compilation in one volume, came out in 1805, the year before he died.

Sheraton's first work, the *Drawing Book*, is by far his most important, and it is important for its drawings. Sheraton was no great shakes as an author but he was an excellent draughtsman and the full notes to the plates reveal that he did have technical experience. Some 600 cabinet-makers and joiners

The Sheraton chair

were among the subscribers to the work which was a brilliant summary of 'the present taste in furniture'.

Shipping Goods Trade term applied to articles, usually late Victorian or Edwardian, bought in bulk by wholesale buyers from overseas. A superior class of shipping trade is that between British dealers and buyers from the antiques departments of large overseas stores who seek 'furnishing antiques' (q.v.).

Shiraz Rugs Persian, of medium weave, both the Ghiordiz and Senna knot used; typical designs are the hexagonal medallion and cone device; red is the basic colour.

Shirvan Rugs Caucasian, Ghiordiz knot, loose texture and coarse weave. The ivory ground is favoured with geometrical designs—medallions, diamonds, stars—in red, blue, green and brown. Three to five stripe border.

Shu Fu Porcelain Ware made at Ching-tê-chên during the Yüan and early Ming dynasties, mostly dishes and bowls with incised, moulded or slip decoration under a pale blue-green or blue-white glaze; some pieces bear the incised inscription *shu fu*, or *fu*, or *lu*. Also known as *Privy Council* ware.

Shoe-piece Until about 1700 the splat of a chair back was not connected with the seat. But for most of the eighteenth century the splat did come down to the seat and the shaped projection into which the splat bedded was termed a 'shoe-piece'.

Shouldered Stem *See* **Silesian Stem.**

Shovel- or Shuffle-board Table Long (very long), narrow table made for the game of 'shovillaborde' in the fifteenth, sixteenth and seventeenth centuries.

Sideboard The sideboard proper, as distinct from the dining-room side-table, dates from the early years of George III's reign. At first detached pedestals, supporting urns, flanked the side-table; a little later the pedestals became connected with the board and drawers were fitted to the frieze. During the Regency period the pedestal type returned to fashion, but the proportions were ill-considered.

Silesian Glass   Glass made in Silesia; rivalled the products of Bohemia, particularly in the seventeenth and eighteenth centuries, and is noted for the engraved glass made during the eighteenth century.

Silesian Stem   A style of drinking glass stem, with a shoulder, which may be spiral-moulded or vertically ribbed or reeded; early examples are frequently four-sided. Often called the *shouldered* or *moulded pedestal* stem. Popular throughout the first half of the eighteenth century.

Sivas Rugs   Rare type of Asia Minor rug from the city of Sivas; noted for white field with red medallion and blue, white, green and yellow floral corners; not very bright; fine cotton for both warp and weft is unusual feature.

Skewer   Silver examples are esteemed mainly because they make good letter-openers.

Skillet   Forerunner of the modern saucepan and successor of the cauldron, a small metal pot with long handle and (usually) legs. Except for some rare, early, bronze skillets the most esteemed are silver examples of the seventeenth century, especially if they are complete with cover.

Skirt   The apron, or strip of wood beneath the front of the seat of a chair.

Sleigh Bed   Bed of the Empire period, without posts but with head and foot boards rolling over.

Slider   *See* **Coaster.**

Slip   Clay reduced to liquid and used variously for the decoration of pottery. It may be white or coloured. The most common use is to form a first coating.

Slipware   Pottery decorated with slip (q.v.).

Snake Foot   Foot splaying out like a snake's head.

Snake Wood   Red Brazilian wood with black markings like snakeskin; used for marquetry.

Snaphaunce   A type of gunlock invented in the Netherlands during the sixteenth century. Some experts hold the snaphaunce to be the earliest form of flintlock; others contend that it is a distinct type from which the flintlock developed. But basically the snaphaunce comprises a piece of flint held in the jaws of a cock for striking against a piece of steel to cause sparks. When the steel is knocked back by the cock the separate sliding cover of the pan is opened and the sparks can get to the priming.

Snuff Bottle   Chinese bottle to contain snuff or medicine with stopper-spoon; those made during the Chien Lung period are very fine.

Snuff Box   Dates from the seventeenth century and is to be found in gold, silver, brass, pewter, steel, tortoiseshell, porcelain, wood, papier mâché, ivory, pinchbeck, horn. . . . Enamel examples from Battersea (particularly) and Bilston are esteemed but have been faked a lot. The small pocket snuff box would hold from quarter to half an ounce; larger boxes, often with detachable lids, were meant for the table; the latter, if long enough to take cigarettes, are much sought and correspondingly expensive. Snuff boxes with incorporated rasps went out towards the end of the eighteenth century with the advent of prepared snuff.

Snuff Spoon   Small, usually of silver; for the use of ladies who did not want to get the snuff under their nails.

Snuffers   Implement for shortening the wick of a candle (which was not fully consumed by the flame until the nineteenth century). Snuffers are mentioned in the fifteenth century. From the post-Restoration period onward they consist of two hinged blades, one fitted with a box, the other with a plate or blade which is pressed into the box when the candle is snuffed (not unlike a pair of scissors).

Snuffer Stand   Upright holder for snuffers (*see* above).

Snuffer Tray   Vertical holder for snuffers; superseded the stand (*see* above) in the eighteenth century.

Soaprock or Soapstone   Steatite which in its natural state contains china clay and is therefore helpful in the manufacture of porcelain. Quarried in Cornwall, it was first used at Bristol (q.v.) about 1748, then at Worcester and other factories.

Sofa   The term appears in the late years of the seventeenth century, and was used to describe 'a couch for reclining' in 1692; it was applied to a long upholstered piece of furniture. In the Regency and Empire period a version of the classical couch was designed and called a 'Grecian sofa'.

Sofa Table   Rectangular, usually with hinged end-leaves, often with two shallow front drawers: an extremely elegant

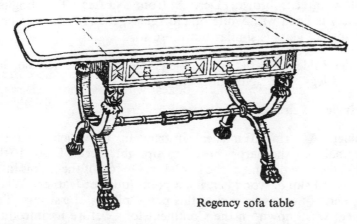

Regency sofa table

table that dates from the late Georgian period and found high favour with the Regency.

177

Soffit The underside of a cornice or lintel. An architectural term carried over into furniture.

Soft-paste Porcelain *See* **Porcelain.**

Solon, Marc French ceramic artist who worked at Sèvres before coming to England in 1871 to work for Mintons, bringing the *pâte-sur-pâte* (q.v.) technique with him.

Soumak Rugs Caucasian, no pile (a tapestry stitch being used), most designs are geometrical, particularly large diamonds with accompanying flattened octagons; red, blue and brown are the usual colours, and the border may have two to five stripes.

Spandrel The space between the outer curve of an arch and the rectangle formed by enclosing moulding.

Spandrel Pieces Cast brass ornaments affixed to the spaces outside the hour-ring in clock faces, dating from the Restoration period to the middle years of the eighteenth century.

Spatter Glass Vivid, mottled with bright colours—red, yellow, green, brown. Derives from Nailsea. The English variety is lined with white opaque glass; the American is not. 'Spangled' glass is similar but more so.

Spider Table A variety of gate-leg table with extremely slender turned legs; mid-eighteenth century.

Spindle A fire rod or baluster.

Spinet A stringed musical instrument in which, like the virginal and the harpsichord, an upright piece of wood (the jack) rests on the end of the key lever. On top of the jack is inset a pivoted slip of wood bearing a point (quill or leather). When the end of the key lever rises this point 'plucks' the strings. The spinet was known on the Continent long before its introduction into England about the middle of the seventeenth century, when it replaced the virginal and remained in favour for about

100 years until it was replaced in its turn by the small piano. Strictly the spinet should be of 'trapezond, pentagonal or wing-shape' as opposed to the virginal which is of rectangular form.

Spinning Wheel A machine with a revolving wheel operated by a treadle, for converting wool, flax or cotton into thread. Generally of wood, the spinning wheel dates back to the fourteenth century (perhaps earlier) and was still in use at the end of the eighteenth century.

Spiral Turning Turned work in the form of a twist.

Splad or Splat Central section of a chair back from top rail to seat.

Spode This ceramics factory founded in 1770 by Josiah Spode I (who had been apprenticed to Thomas Whieldon). On his death in 1797 the business was carried on by his son Josiah Spode II, and later by his grandson Josiah Spode III, who took William Copeland as a partner. From 1833 the firm was known as Copeland & Garrett, and from 1847 Copeland late Spode, and to this day it remains in the Copeland family.

Spode is usually credited with evolving the bone-china body that is still the staple manufacture today. From 1800 extremely large quantities of this porcelain were produced in many styles—the Chinese, Meissen, early Worcester and Derby, Chelsea. Rich ground colours were favoured. Gilding was all too often overdone, especially in the middle of the nineteenth century. Excellent Parian and lustre wares were made. Probably the most prolific English factory, Spode never suffered the reversals which beset so many of their competitors. Their 'stone china' should be mentioned.

Marks usually include the name 'Spode' in some form or other, most often transfer-printed.

Spool Turning Turned work in form of a succession of spools.

Spoon The spoon consists of three parts, the bowl, the stem, and the end or knop (though a form like the 'Puritan' has no knop or finial). Some types that interest collectors: (1) the *Maidenhead* spoon, which appears at the close of the fourteenth century and has as finial a female bust; (2) the *acorn-knop*, mentioned as early as 1346, and made until the early seventeenth century; (3) the *diamond point*, which appeared in the mid-fourteenth century and was still being made in the early seventeenth century; (4) *slipped-top* (i.e. without a knop), mentioned in 1498 and still being made in the second half of the seventeenth century; (5) the *seal top*, introduced about 1525 and remaining in favour till the late seventeenth century; (6) the *Puritan spoon*, which has a flat stem and no knop, introduced in the 1630's and in favour for the remainder of the century; (7) the *trifid spoon* (or lobed end), introduced early in the reign of Charles II and remaining in favour until Anne's accession; (8) *apostle spoons*, in sets surmounted by a figure of an Apostle as knop. The earliest known example bears the mark for 1478. Some sets of twelve are surmounted by figures of the twelve Apostles; others in sets of thirteen (very rare) include the figure of the 'Master' (Christ).

Generally speaking the bowl of the spoon is pear-shaped, narrowest near the stem, until the mid-seventeenth century, when it becomes more oval and then widest near the handle. Marks were placed inside the bowl till about 1660, after which they begin to appear on the handle but near the bowl, and from about 1780 on the handle but near the end.

Spoon-back   Chair back shaped to fit occupant. An American term (?).

Sprimont, Nicholas   One of the founders of the Chelsea porcelain factory, of which he was probably manager from the beginning and owner from about 1757 to 1768. Sprimont was born at Liége and trained as a silversmith, which craft he probably followed when he came to London.

Springs   Not used in upholstered furniture before the nineteenth century.

Stalker and Parker   Their *Treatise on Japanning and Varnishing* was published in 1688, and contained hints not only on japanning and varnishing but also on 'Guilding, Burnishing and Lackering . . . Painting Mezzo-Tinto-Prints . . . Counterfeiting Tortoiseshell, and Marble' and many other secret arts.

Standard Obsolete term for a type of coffer or chest covered with leather.

Standing Cup Richly ornamented ceremonial cup with cover.

Standing Salt A large salt, often of precious metal, which occupied an important position on the dining-table in the Middle Ages and indeed till the beginning of the seventeenth century.

Standish A term that dates from the fifteenth century to describe a stand made to hold inkwell, quills, and other writing materials and accessories. (The term 'inkstand' came into use in the late eighteenth century.)

Steatite *See* **Soaprock.**

Stecco (Italian=stickwork) The term used in Italy for the form of ceramic decoration known in England by the Italian term *sgraffito* (q.v.).

Sterling Term derived from the German tribe, the Easterlings, makers of fine silver in medieval times. Applied as the normal standard of English silver, 925 parts fine, at the beginning of the fourteenth century and has so remained, except for the period 1697–1720 (*see* **Britannia Standard**), to the present time.

Stile The vertical member of a framework, occupying an end position in that framework, into which the rails are tenoned.

Stirrup Cup A drinking cup in the form of a fox's head, though occasionally the form is that of some other animal's head. The stirrup cup is footless and lacks handles. Silver examples were popular sporting trophies. They were also made of pottery and porcelain.

Stitched-up Term applied to upholstery completely covering seat to lower edge of frame.

Stoneware Pottery fused into a hard, vitrified mass, a stage between earthenware and porcelain. Stoneware is always opaque and therefore cannot qualify, in European eyes, as porcelain; but in China, where the criterion is that the ware 'rings' when struck, some stoneware is deemed to be porcelain.

Stool A term used in the Middle Ages for a seat for one person, especially one without arms or back (its usual significance from the Tudor period). In the *Academy of Armory* (1649) joint stools, so called because made by the joiner, are distinguished from turned stools made by the turner or wheelwright. Until the second half of the seventeenth century stools were the normal seats for the dining table.

Storr, Paul London silversmith active 1795–1821; a superb craftsman and the probable begetter of the Regency style as regards silver.

Strapwork Ornament consisting of flat bands interlaced with various patterns such as foliage and flowers, mostly used on furniture (carved), but borrowed by the silversmith. Dates from the middle of the sixteenth century.

Strasbourg Important faience centre in Alsace, which became prominent from *c.* 1720 thanks to a factory established by a partnership between Charles François Hannong and Johann Heinrich Wackenfeld. Wackenfeld, who may have been at Meissen, did not stay long but the enterprise expanded under the direction of Hannong, and later under his son, Joseph. until a decline set in about 1760 and the factory closed in 1780, Important pieces in the rococo style were produced here; and some porcelain was made, the early wares being difficult to distinguish from those of Frankenthal (q.v.).

Straw-work A form of furniture decoration employing strips of straw, bleached and dyed, applied in geometrical or other patterns. This fashion reached England from the Continent towards the end of the seventeenth century and remained popular for well over 100 years (French prisoners-of-war *c.* 1795–1815 produced a great deal of straw-work).

Stretcher Horizontal member between legs of a chair, table or stool.

Stringing A line or narrow band (usually of wood) inlaid as a decorative border on furniture. This practice dates from the second half of the sixteenth century, when light-coloured woods were used to contrast against a darker ground; brass stringing is frequent feature of Regency furniture.

Sung Dynasty (A.D. 960–1279) *See* **Chinese.**

Surfeit Water Glass Delicate flute-shaped drinking glass, the brim less than one inch in diameter; mid-Georgian. (Surfeit water was a fearfully strong brandy.)

Sutherland Table Dwarf table with flap leaves and pull-out leg supports. Name derives from Harriet, Duchess of S. Victorian successor to sofa table.

Swag A festoon of cloth, or of flowers and fruit, favoured as a decorative motif.

Swan-neck Pediment Broken pediment in which the two sides are curved instead of straight.

Swansea (1) PORCELAIN. In 1814 William Billingsley quit his Nantgarw (q.v.) factory and joined forces with Lewis Dillwyn at the latter's Cambrian Pottery works at Swansea, the object being to make an economic success of Billingsley's porcelain

SWANSEA

 Swansea china marks

formula. The enterprise was but a limited success and by 1817 Billingsley was on the move again. Porcelain continued to be made at Swansea till 1823.

The first wares made were very similar to Nantgarw; then

came a more stable body, the 'duck egg' paste, which contained a small amount of soaprock; and later again a harder, whiter porcelain was made, which contained considerably more soaprock. After Billingsley's departure the porcelain made was inferior. The best Swansea is as good—and as rare—as Nantgarw. Table ware, plates particularly, was the main product. Painted decoration by Thomas Baxter, Thomas Pardoe and William Young is highly esteemed. 'SWANSEA' usually impressed but sometimes painted in red or other colours, is the standard mark.

Swansea (2) POTTERY. The Cambrian Pottery works was founded during the 1760's and remained in the Coles family until 1802 when it passed to Lewis Dillwyn. It traded as Bevington & Co. for a time, then reverted to Dillwyn about 1823, finally passing into other hands and closing down in 1870.

Swell Front Bow front.

Sycamore Yellowish wood, fine-grained, medium-hard, takes an excellent polish; was used for marquetry on walnut furniture, and as veneer and in the solid during the last third of the eighteenth century when the vogue was for satinwood furniture.

Table The earliest form of table was of trestle construction in which the top could be readily dismantled. The *joined* table, in which the main underframe is tenoned into the tops of the legs, first came into use in England at the beginning of the sixteenth century. For various types of tables, *see* under such entries as **Gate-leg, Pembroke, Rent, Work,** etc.

Tabouret (French) A low seat or stool. Upholstered examples were often made to match a *bergère* (q.v.) chair.

Tabriz Carpets Persian, of fine weave; Ghiordiz knot; fine, short wool pile. The best Tabriz carpets and rugs are of extremely high quality being noted for graceful designs of cnrved medallions and scrolls; animals and birds are sometimes incorporated. The main colours: red, blue, green, ivory.

Five to eight stripe border. Beautiful silk carpets are sometimes encountered.

Tallboy A chest-on-chest that evolved out of the chest-on-stand in the early eighteenth century.

Tambour Narrow strips of wood glued side by side to stout canvas to form sliding doors in cabinets and sideboards, and sliding roll-top covers to late eighteenth-century writing desks.

T'ang Dynasty (A.D. 618–906) *See* **Chinese.** -

Tankard Originally a drinking vessel of wooden staves hooped together, but now the term applies to a one-handled mug, drum-like, of pewter or silver, usually fitted with a lid.

Tapestry A hand-woven fabric in which the pattern is woven on a loom. Of the two weaving systems, in the *haute lisse* (high warp) the loom is upright and the leashes are worked by hand, whereas in the *basse lisse* (low warp) the loom is horizontal and the leashes are operated by heddles and treadles. In the Middle Ages, Arras (q.v.) and Bruges were great tapestry centres; in the seventeenth and eighteenth centuries the French factories —Gobelins, Beauvais, Savonnerie, Aubusson (qq.v.)—were supreme. Mortlake, a factory that flourished *c.* 1620–1700, is the only English manufactory that can be mentioned in company with the foregoing names.

Tarsia *See* **Intarsia.**

Taws Balls made of pottery and used in the game of carpet bowls.

Tazza Shallow-bowled drinking cup.

Tea-caddy A small box for holding tea, known as a 'tea chest' until the late eighteenth century. Often made of fine woods and delicately finished, tea-caddies were made in various shapes, inlaid, plain, lacquered Some caddies are divided into interior compartments lined with pewter (two usually; one for black and one for green tea); others were intended to hold canisters for different kinds of tea.

Tea-canister Container for tea which was itself contained in the tea-caddy (*see* above); made of glass, metal, pottery, occasionally silver.

Teak Dark brown wood from India and Burma; very strong and durable and heavy; it was used in the eighteenth century in England but its weight told against it.

Teapot The earliest known English silver teapot (1670) is inscribed 'tea pott'; but for this inscription the vessel would probably be taken for a coffee-pot, for there was no difference in their form at first. Towards the end of the seventeenth century a squat form copied from Chinese hot water pots of porcelain began to appear. During the first quarter of the eighteenth century a pear-shaped body with a high domed lid was usual; then a globular body and moulded base was the rule till the last quarter of the eighteenth century, when an oval body with a straight spout came into fashion. When porcelain came into favour in the second half of the eighteenth century it was of course quickly adopted for teapots.

Teapoy At first (mid-eighteenth century) a small three-legged individual table on which tea was served; later the tea-caddy stood on it and later still, from about 1812, became one with it to form a pedestal table with lifting top in which tea was kept. Papier mâché much used from the 1840's.

Tebo Mr Tebo is a rather mysterious figure linked with the T° mark that has been found on porcelain produced at Bow, Worcester, Plymouth and possibly Bristol. Some figures so marked are remarkably well modelled.

Tê-hua porcelain A type of Chinese porcelain made at Tê-hua in Fukien Province; the best examples are of superb quality, extremely translucent. Sometimes known as *blanc-de-chine*, the whiteness of this porcelain ranges from almost bluish

The silver tea pot.
1, 1716. 2, 1731.
3, 1805. 4, 1820.
5, 1777

chalk-white to cream. Small figures of Buddha and the like are typical and European figures are encountered. (Ming.)

Temmoku (Japanese) *See* **Chien Ware.**

Tenon *See* **Mortise and Tenon.**

Terracotta (Italian=baked earth) Red earthenware.

Term Pedestal stand in the form of a human bust (usually of a child or a woman).

Terre de Pipe (French=pipe clay) The term applies to the products of some French faience factories. The paste has a hard white quality and is covered with a very thin transparent glaze.

Tester A term used in the sixteenth century for the canopy of a bed. In the case of four-poster beds, the tester is the wooden ceiling supported by the headboard and the posts.

Throwing Early term for turning.

Tiger-ware Jug English term for German salt-glazed stoneware jug as imported into England in the sixteenth century. These jugs are round-bellied and with a cylindrical neck. The name derives from the brown mottled glaze.

Till A tray or shallow drawer, especially as fitted in a medieval chest or in presses and cupboards in the sixteenth and seventeenth centuries.

Tin-enamel or Tin Glaze Lead glaze, rendered opaque by the addition of oxide of tin, used on pottery. *Delft, faience* and *maiolica* (qq.v.) are tin-enamelled.

Ting (Chinese) Ancient, three-footed (sometimes four) bronze cooking vessel. Usually circular in shape, with two handles standing up from the rim. Rectangular examples are known.

Ting Ware Porcelain of the Sung period made originally at Ting Chou, Chihli Province, and later (after 1127) in the district of Chi Chou, Kiangsi Province—hence the terms 'northern Ting' for the earlier product and 'southern Ting' for the later, though it is almost impossible to distinguish one from the other. The body is white with an orange-tinted translucency and the glaze may be cream or ivory white or, on a coarser ware, yellowish. Decoration is carved or impressed under the glaze. Vessels were fired upside down and thus the lip is unglazed and sometimes mounted with a band of copper.

Toasting Glass A firing glass (q.v.), but there was a distinct type of toasting glass (early Georgian) made with an extremely slender stem that could be snapped between finger and thumb —for the special occasion. Because of their nature few if any have survived.

Toast-master Glass Drinking glass of ordinary appearance but with deceptive bowl that holds only a thimbleful of liquid. From about 1750.

Toby Jug Pottery jug made in the form of a seated man holding a mug and a clay pipe. This is the basic form; there are, of course, variations. The first maker may well have been Ralph Wood (q.v.). Genuine old Toby jugs have hollow legs and feet and are much lighter in weight than one might expect.

Toddy Rummer A large, strong, glass vessel in which hot toddy was prepared; made from the 1780's; too heavy and awkward to drink from with any ease. The bowls usually engraved with considerable artistry and skill.

Toft, Thomas Seventeenth century Staffordshire potter. Surviving pieces by Toft are few (and mostly in museums) but are identifiable by his marked name and his style of slip-decoration.

Toilet Mirror *See* **Mirrors** for an introduction to the subject. Mirrors for the dressing table seem to have been first made in England about the time of the Restoration; the fashion came from France. They were usually square in shape, decorated with stump-work, and were frequently supported by means of a hinged strut at the back. A mirror was normally included in the toilet sets that came in after the Restoration.

The toilet mirror, or dressing glass, mounted on a stand came into favour at the beginning of the eighteenth century. The framed glass swivelled between uprights and the stand or base was fitted with drawers and compartments to hold toilet requisites. The head of the mirror is usually arched in Queen Anne and George I examples and the favoured wood was walnut. The use of mahogany became usual about 1745 but the design changed but little till the classical revival when it became simpler and the frame and glass was likely to be oval or shield shaped. By 1800 the shape became squarish again but of greater width than height. The last quarter of the eighteenth century saw the introduction of the full-length cheval dressing glass (q.v.).

Tompion, Thomas (1640–1713)   The greatest of English clockmakers; son of a Bedfordshire blacksmith, he so prospered as to die a rich man and be buried in Westminster Abbey. The date of his coming to London is not known, but he entered the Clockmakers' Company in 1671 (when he was thirty-one) as a fully qualified craftsman. He was not one of the great innovators; his pre-eminence lies in his all-round excellence, his exquisite craftsmanship, his natural good taste. His cases are usually simple and clean-lined and beautifully proportioned.

Torchère (French)   A similar piece of furniture to the *guéridon* (q.v.) but taller.

Tortoiseshell   The shell or scales of the tortoise has the useful property of becoming plastic when heated and retaining a desired shape when cooled. Its use as a furniture veneer was common in Holland and some other European countries during the seventeenth century, but in England it was little if at all used until after the introduction of Boulle (q.v.) furniture.

Touch   Pewterer's mark (usually the maker's initials).

Tournai Porcelain first produced at this Belgian factory in 1751; in 1752 the name of *Manufacture Imperiale et Royale* was adopted. Excellent Sèvres-like porcelain was made; during the nineteenth century the wares of Chelsea and Worcester were imitated a lot. Crossed swords with four tiny crosses are a common mark, as is a tower. (There is a class of modern fakes, very thin in the body, that is marked with a large tower.)

Train Horological term for the series of wheels and pinions which, geared together, form the mechanism of a clock or watch; e.g. chiming train, going train, striking train.

Transfer Printing This technique of decorating pottery and porcelain seems to have been an English invention and is largely confined to English wares. It dates from the 1750's. The method involves inking an engraved copper plate and taking a paper print from this; while the ink is still wet the impression is transferred from the paper to the ware; the paper is then soaked off and the coloured design fixed by firing. (*See* **Bat-printing**.) Early users of the process: Battersea Enamel Works, Bow, Worcester, Sadler & Green of Liverpool.

Transylvanian Rugs From Transylvania but originating in Asia Minor and of intriguing interest to the specialist with their seventeenth century dark fields and arabesques and colours in spandrels and corners, then their eighteenth century Turkish and more simplified designs. Most common later specimens have ivory fields and motifs in red and brown, three-stripe border and coarse weaves.

Tray Sheraton in his *Cabinet Dictionary* (1803) defines trays as 'boards with rims round them, on which to place glasses, plates, and a tea equipage', but in medieval times the tray, or 'voyder' as it was then called, was used mainly for the removal of dirty dishes and scraps from the dining table. Few trays survive from earlier than the mid-eighteenth century. Pierced or lattice-work rims were popular. In the first edition of Chippendale's *Director* (1754) there are several designs for 'tea-trays or voiders'. Later in the eighteenth century much more ornamentation (such as marquetry) is introduced. In the late eighteenth and early nineteenth centuries *papier mâché* trays and trays of japanned metal were manufactured in quantities in Birmingham. Trays of silver survive from the end of the seventeenth century, some superbly chased and engraved.

Treen   Articles of wood, small domestic objects such as bowls, spoons.

Trencher   Plate of wood, and later of pewter.

Trencher Salt   Small open salt cellar introduced in the second quarter of the seventeenth century; often in sets.

Trestle   Table-top support consisting of solid shaped ends secured to massive feet and usually held in position by stretcher beams.

Trestle Table   A long table supported by trestles, the normal dining table from the Middle Ages until the introduction of the joined table in the sixteenth century.

Tric-trac Board   Tric-trac is a form of backgammon; boards, very decorative some of them, survive from the seventeenth century.

Tridarn   Welsh variety of the three-stage cupboard or press; the top stage is open and is often removable.

Trifle   Common pewter, 83 parts tin to 17 antimony.

Tripod   Three-footed support which came into use for English furniture in the early eighteenth century.

Trivet   Metal stand on which to place a pot or kettle or other vessel beside the fire. The usual form has three legs and a projecting handle and often a curved top, but four-legged examples with rectangular tops are to be found, and a quite different type is the hanging trivet which is attached to the top bar of the grate.

Trompe l'Oeil The painting of objects with such clarity and realism that they might be the things themselves rather than representations.

Truckle Bed Small bed which could be pushed under a larger bed.

Tsuba (Japanese) Sword-guard, often elaborately decorated.

Tulip Wood A heavy hard wood, light-coloured with reddish stripes, from the West Indies and Brazil. Used in England for marquetry and veneer in the second half of the eighteenth century.

Tumbler A straight-sided, stemless drinking glass, formerly with a rounded base.

Tumblers *See* **Locks.**

Tunbridge ware Place-name given to a marquetry veneer so microscopic and detailed it has been called the 'English mosaic'; from late eighteenth century (though some would say from the late seventeenth century; but the early evolution of the ware is obscure), with the nineteenth century the heyday. Designs are frequently geometrical; the elongated triangle, the diamond and the parallelogram are typical. Many, many woods were used, the important thing was that they be colourful and have attractive graining.

Turkey Work Upholstery, cushions and carpets knotted, in the manner of Turkish rugs, to form a pile. Turkey work was practised and so-called in England from the early sixteenth to the middle of the eighteenth century.

Turned Chair Chair of which the members of the legs and back consist of turned work.

Turner, John Staffordshire potter of Stoke and Lane End, active 1755–82, noted for his white stoneware, cream-coloured earthenware, and his jasper particularly. He was a founder-member of the New Hall Porcelain Company. The Lane End factory was continued by his sons, John and William, until the early years of the nineteenth century.

Turner, Thomas Proprietor of the Caughley porcelain factory (q.v.).

Turnings Lathe-turned wood.

Turquerie Objects in the Turkish style—cf. *Chinoiserie*.

Tutenag Zinc; but *see* **Paktong**.

Tyg A many-handled drinking vessel.

Tz'u Chou Ware Stoneware made at Tz'u Chou (which is now in Chihli Province) since the Sung dynasty. The porcellaneous body is pale grey or yellowish-grey, with slip decoration usually, and covered with a transparent glaze. The *sgraffito* technique (incising the design through the slip on to the body) was also used. Both technically and artistically Tz'u Chou wares are of a high order.

Unaker China clay from America. 'The material is an earth, the produce of the Cherokee nation in America, called by the natives, Unaker' (The Heylyn and Frye patent of 1744). This clay may have been used at Bow; Cookworthy knew about it, as did Champion; samples were tested at Worcester.

Under-brace Stretcher.

Underglaze Decoration applied to pottery and porcelain in its biscuit state before the application of the glaze.

Upholder The old name for an upholsterer.

Upholstery Textile or leather covering, padded and/or sprung, for furniture. Upholstery was in early times confined to beds, hangings and cushions. But by the sixteenth century upholstered furniture was coming in to its own with the use of such materials as hide, ornamental leather, velvet, satin, tapestry and needlework. Fringed upholstery was a feature of the Jacobean and Carolean periods when padded seats first came into general use.

Urn Classically-shaped vase, two-handled and with domed cover. The urn was used as a decorative finial (q.v.) on furniture in the eighteenth century.

Urn Stand A small table to take the tea kettle or urn (sometimes with an accompanying small slide on which to place the teapot); eighteenth century.

'Useful Wares' Term often used of ceramic wares to indicate that they were made for use rather than for ornament.

Varnish Resinous solution applied to wood to give a hard, shiny, transparent coat. Oil varnish was used in England until the introduction of spirit varnish towards the end of the seventeenth century. 'French polish' came to England from France in the 1820's. *See* **Japanning, Lacquer, Polish.**

Veneer The gluing down of thin sheets of wood on to a carcase. The process dates from the second half of the seventeenth century. As the veneers had to be cut by a hand-saw the sheets were seldom less than one-eighth of an inch thick. The best veneers were costly; to achieve rich effects timber was cut at wasteful angles, while the matching of designs on the finished work also led to much waste.

Venice Porcelain A hard-paste porcelain factory was founded *c.* 1720 in Venice by Francesco Vezzi with the aid of a workman who had been at Meissen and Vienna, and the influence of these two factories is to be discerned in the wares produced. This factory probably closed in 1728. The word 'Venezia' or an abbreviation of it is the mark. Another, shorter-lived Venetian factory was that founded *c.* 1758 by N. F. Hewelcke of Dresden; it closed in 1763; the mark is the letter v. In 1764 a third factory was established by Geminiano Cozzi and seems to have been more successful. At any rate it survived until 1812. The mark is an anchor.

Vermeil (French)   Silver-gilt.

Vernis Martin   A term embracing most varnishes and lacquers used in the decoration of fans, small boxes, furniture, even carriages. In the mid-eighteenth century the brothers Martin obtained a monopoly to make lacquer in relief in the Chinese and Japanese style. The brothers, Simon-Etienne, Julien and Robert, did not invent a lacquer, but they developed and' improved various coloured and translucent varnishes. There were three factories in Paris directed by them.

Verre Églomise (French)   Glass decorated on the reverse side and backed with metal foil. The process is very old, much, much older than the Frenchman Glomy (died 1786) whose name it bears. The glass borders of mirrors were decorated by this process at the end of the seventeenth century and later.

Verroterie Cloisonné   *See* **Cell-glazing**.

Verzelini, Giacomo (1522–1606)   Venetian who taught the English how to make fine table glass, thus breaking the Venetian monopoly; working, London, from early 1570's to 1592; glass-maker to Queen Elizabeth I.

Vetro di Trina   Italian, lace-like glass, the finest work in the *latticino* (q.v.) technique.

Vienna porcelain   The factory founded in 1719. For a few years before this a Viennese court official, Claudius Innocentius Du Paquier, had attempted to make porcelain but it was not until he obtained the help of two workmen from Meissen that he succeeded. These workmen soon left him but Du Paquier went on making excellent porcelain until he was forced to sell the factory to the State in 1744. In this first period the early wares are often in the Chinese manner, but later European subjects come into favour and some very beautiful Baroque porcelain was made. During the second period, 1744–84, under various directors appointed by the State, figures and groups are notable and wares were made in imitation of Sèvres. The normal Vienna mark, an incised shield, was introduced in 1744. Financial difficulties caused the factory to be offered for

 Vienna china marks

sale again, but no buyer could be found. Then Konrad von Sorgenthal took over as director in 1784 and brought the concern back to prosperity, thanks mainly to his famous table-wares with neo-classical decoration of great beauty and refinement. On Sorgenthal's death in 1805 a decline set in, although the factory did not close till 1864.

Vile, William (?–1767)   Cabinet-maker who, in the 1750's and 60's, was perhaps the finest craftsman of his day. As he was in partnership with John Cobb (q.v.) it is difficult to ascribe individual pieces to Vile with certainty; but most experts agree that Vile was not only the senior partner but also by far the superior craftsman.

Vinaigrette (from French *vinaigre*, vinegar)   Small gold or silver box, with hinged lid, containing aromatic sponge. Dates from eighteenth century; grew larger and more ornate in Victorian times; ousted by smelling salts at end of nineteenth century.

Vincennes   This soft-paste porcelain factory founded in 1738 and transferred to Sèvres in 1756. *See* **Sèvres.**

Vinovo   Porcelain factory situated near Turin, founded in 1776 and though it did not finally close till about 1820 there were lengthy closures between those dates. The French style predominated. The mark is usually a cross surmounting the letter 'v'.

Virginal   Small musical instrument, rectangular in shape, which has the same basic mechanism as the spinet (q.v.).

Examples are rare. The name is said to derive from the fact that the instrument was extremely popular with ladies (and in convents), and because of this it was called a 'clavicordium virginale'. The harpsichord (q.v.) seems to have evolved out of the virginal in the fifteenth century.

Vitrine (French) ˙A display cabinet with glass door and sides.

Vitruvian Scroll Ornament consisting of a series of repeating wave-like scrolls; architectural, but used on furniture, especially during the classical revival at the end of the eighteenth century.

Volkstedt A porcelain factory founded at Volkstedt, Thuringia, *c.* 1760; both soft- and hard-paste porcelain was made, but like most of the Thuringian factories the wares produced here were greyish and coarse.

Volute A spiral scroll found particularly on an Ionic capital.

Voyder A large dish or tray (medieval).

Voyez, John Ceramics modeller of distinction who worked for Wedgwood, Humphrey Palmer, Ralph Wood and on his own account; active 1767–90. 'Fair Hebe' jugs are associated with this maker.

Vulliamy Family of London clock-makers of renown who practised their craft in London from *c.* 1740–1850.

Wag-on-the-wall clock Of Dutch origin (the Friesland Clock), for hanging on the wall; long exposed pendulum and weights.

Wainscot (from the Low German *wagenshot*) Originally the term was used to describe a consignment of timber from the Baltic, by the seventeenth century the word was used to describe timber for use in furniture and panelling and it is this latter reference that has survived.

Waiter A small silver tray dating from the eighteenth century.

Waldglas   A glass made in Germany during the Middle Ages, green, brown, yellow; sometimes called 'Natural Forest Glass' because the alkali came from ferns and bracken.

Walnut   There are two varieties. The first, grown in Europe (including England) and some eastern countries, is pale brown with dark brown and black veining. The other, sometimes called 'Virginia' or 'black' walnut, is of a deep brown colour with dark markings and veining; it comes from the eastern states of the U.S.A. Walnut is an excellent carving wood and it takes a good finish. It was used in the solid in France and Italy during the Renaissance, but in England the 'age of walnut' is 1660–1720.

Wardrobe   Developed from the oak cupboard or press during the eighteenth century. Early wardrobes are not usually made with doors the full height, but have a hanging section above a tier (or tiers) of drawers. Large wardrobes dating from the middle of the eighteenth century are constructed in three sections, the centre forming a case of drawers or clothes press, the wings serving as hanging cupboards.

Warming Pan   Originally a covered metal pan enclosed in a wooden cage. In the fifteenth century the cage was dispensed with and a long handle was attached to the pan. The best are of brass, finely-pierced, and with iron handles.

Washing Stand   A stand specifically designed to hold a basin does not seem to have been made before the middle of the eighteenth century. In the second half of that century several types evolved, notably the 'disguised' type which, when closed, looked like a small table or chest of drawers, the circular tripod basin-stand, usually with a small central shelf or drawer, and another type with so many fittings, including a mirror, that it almost qualifies as a dressing table.

Waster   Porcelain spoilt in the firing so that when taken from the kiln it has to be thrown away.

Watch   The invention of the portable clock or watch goes back to the early sixteenth century. Germany took an early lead in watch-making, Nuremberg being famous for its watches, and later the industry was established in France, and at Geneva by 1585. The so-called 'Nuremberg eggs' (q.v.), of flattened oval form, were made in the south of Germany between c. 1600–50. The first glasses were fitted to watches about 1600; prior to 1700 watches had one hand only. Few if any English watches were made before 1600.

Waterford Glass Some glass seems to have been made at Waterford from the second quarter of the eighteenth century but it was not till the 1780's that activities became remarkable. In England the Glass Excise Act of 1745, which taxed flint glass by weight, discouraged the making of heavy glass. Ireland could not at first take much advantage of this owing to export restrictions; but in 1780 Irish glass-makers were allowed full freedom to export, a freedom quickly seized by *English* merchants. John Hill, member of a Stourbridge glass-making family, went to Waterford in 1784, taking more than fifty skilled workmen with him, to manage the Penrose Brothers' Glasshouse. The Penrose brothers relinquished control in 1799, but thanks to Hill, and later Jonathan Gatchell, a world-wide reputation was built up for Waterford cut glassware. A decline set in about 1830 (the glass excise duty imposed in Ireland in 1825 may have had something to do with this) and the glasshouse closed in 1851. Waterford glass has no distinctive features and, unless a stamped seal shows the makers' name, identification is difficult, even for the expert.

Webley revolver The most successful British weapon of its type, still the prominent product of Webley & Scott Ltd., Birmingham, developed from the unique double-action invention of Philip Webley and Robert Adams, 1851.

Wedgwood The great name in Staffordshire pottery. Records of the Wedgwoods, as potters, date back to the early seventeenth century. Josiah Wedgwood (1730–95), the son of Thomas and Mary Wedgwood, was apprenticed as a thrower to his brother Thomas in 1745; by 1754 he had commenced a five-year partnership with Thomas Whieldon; in 1759 he launched out on his own. Ten years later the factory he had built, Etruria, was in production and in that year (1769) his partnership with Thomas Bentley began, a partnership that lasted till Bentley's death in 1780 The business continued to prosper during Wedgwood's lifetime, went into decline under the direction of his son, Josiah Wedgwood II, and subsequently, but is today in high regard again.

Wedgwood experimented from the beginning, certainly from the time he was with Whieldon. He was fortunate in that his creamware, perfected in the early 1760's, soon after he set up on his own, was such a commercial success. It was the bread-and-

Wedgwood jasper vase

butter line that enabled him to devote time and cash to the superb ornamental wares, particularly jasper and basalts (qq.v.), and to such projects as copying the Portland vase (q.v.). The greatest of English potters, Wedgwood's influence on his fellow manufacturers of pottery and porcelain both in Britain and on the Continent was profound.

Marks nearly always include the word 'Wedgwood' although the initials 'w' & B.' (for Wedgwood and Bentley) may be encountered. The inclusion of the Christian name 'Josiah' indicates the period of Josiah Wedgwood II.

Welsh Dresser A side-table or dresser consisting of pot-board, two-doored cupboard, drawers and a shelved upper structure. This is the usual form, though there are variations. Normally of oak.

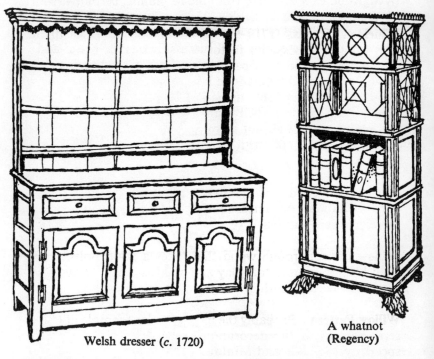

Welsh dresser (*c.* 1720)

A whatnot
(Regency)

Whatnot Square or rectangular stand of three or four tiers with turned, sometimes bobbin-shaped, pillars and drawer beneath; on castors often; of rosewood, mahogany, walnut. Georgian and Regency examples often have ormolu rails; Victorian (the heyday) are sometimes adorned with fretwork.

Wheel-lock Form of gun ignition. The matchlock (q.v.) musket was extremely clumsy, and about 1517 at Nuremberg the wheel-lock was invented—possibly based on the extant fifteenth century designs of Leonardo da Vinci. The wheel employed has a serrated edge and is first 'wound up', then released to spin and make contact with pyrites, thus showering sparks on priming in the pan. Its principal advantage over earlier methods was that a wheel-lock gun could be loaded and carried or left about ready to fire at once. But it was expensive to make.

Whieldon, Thomas (1719–95) Staffordshire potter of distinction who established his factory at Fenton Low in 1740, had Josiah Wedgwood as a partner 1754–59, made every kind of pottery that could be made in his time, and retired a rich man about 1780. Whieldon's name is particularly associated with 'agate' ware, 'tortoiseshell' ware and 'marbled' wares. He also made figures (though not so many as are attributed to him!), simple, lively and colourful. (There are no marks on Whieldon's wares.)

Wig-stand A wooden standard, usually on a circular base, with a bulbous or mushroom-shaped knob at the top. An extremely rare survival.

Willow A soft tough wood that takes a good polish; often dyed black and used for inlay and applied ornament on furniture in the seventeenth and eighteenth centuries.

Willow Pattern Probably the most popular example of chinoiserie applied to the decoration of porcelain in England. A speciality of Spode and Minton.

Wilton Carpets Wilton, Wiltshire, has been noted for its carpets since 1740 when a factory was established as a result of the efforts of the Earl of Pembroke to introduce the Brussels manner of carpet making (woven as velvet). The cutting of the looped pile was probably practised from the beginning. The Axminster (q.v.) looms were acquired in 1835 and since then knotted pile carpets have been made.

Windsor Chair A type of chair with back and legs formed of spindles and turnings inserted in a shaped seat (which is usually of elm). The spindle back surmounted by a top rail was usual till about 1740 when the hoop back came in. Manu-

The Windsor chair

factured chiefly in Buckinghamshire, this type of chair was widely used as a garden chair, and in inns and farmhouses. The woods used were beech, elm, ash or yew.

Wine Cistern An oval or circular vessel, usually on legs, for keeping bottles cool. Wooden cisterns, lead-lined, came in about 1730. Most are of mahogany, often with brass hoops and mounts. Cisterns of metal date from the late seventeenth century.

Wine Cooler A smallish silver vessel for keeping a single bottle cool.

Wine Table A type of table, dating from the late eighteenth century, specifically designed for after dinner drinking. A typical example is horseshoe-shaped and has two metal coasters attached to a brass rod (or sliding in a well).

Wine Waiter A wagon on legs with castors for circulating wines and spirits in a dining room. The top is in effect a partitioned tray. They were made in the second half of the eighteenth century.

Wing Bookcase Another name for the breakfront bookcase.

Wing Chair Upholstered chair with high back and projecting or winged sides, which are sometimes called cheeks, the arms usually ending in a scroll or turnover.

Witch Ball Glass globe, often lustred or otherwise treated to resemble polished silver.

Wood Family of Staffordshire potters, the most famous being Ralph I (active *c.* 1750–70; figures and toby jugs are notable), his son Ralph II and his grandson Ralph III who continued the business till about 1800; Aaron Wood, a brother of Ralph I, was the finest block-cutter of his time and worked for nearly all the leading potters and probably at the Longton Hall porcelain factory; Enoch Wood, a son of Aaron, was active 1783–1840, trading variously as Enoch Wood & Co., Wood and Caldwell, and, from 1818, Enoch Wood & Sons.

Worcester The Worcester 'Tonquin Manufacture' was established in 1751 by a company which included Dr John Wall, Richard and Josiah Holdship. In 1783 the factory was bought by Thomas Flight for his sons, Joseph and John. After the death of John Flight, Barr was taken into partnership in 1792 and from that year until 1840 the firm's style went like this: 1792 to 1807, Flight & Barr; 1807 to 1813, Barr, Flight & Barr;

1813 to 1840, Flight, Barr & Barr. In 1840 Robert Chamberlain's factory was amalgamated with the older company. From 1852 to 1862 the firm traded as Kerr & Binns and from 1862 to the present the correct style is the Royal Worcester Porcelain Company. Two local factories were victims of take-over bids: that of Thomas Grainger in 1889 and that of James Hadley & Sons in 1905.

Early Worcester had a soft-paste body which contained soaprock; it shows greenish when held up to the light and appears somewhat opaque when viewed from a distance. Underglaze blue was a favoured decoration and the usual Oriental influences are apparent. From about 1765 Meissen provides the inspiration, soon (from 1768) to be rivalled by Sèvres. Transfer-printing was much used at Worcester (Robert Hancock was closely associated with the company for a time);

Worcester china marks

painted decoration by such miniaturists as J. H. O'Neale and John Donaldson was of a very high order; a great deal of Worcester porcelain was decorated in the London workshop of James Giles during the 1760's and 70's. Figures were never a speciality at Worcester and are relatively rare.

'Japan' patterns were much used from the early years of the nineteenth century. Figure painting was quite outstanding, as were topographical scenes, but most of the floral decoration was dull. Some pierced wares are esteemed, and the 'egg shell' china produced from the 1850's has many admirers.

Marks are many and varied. Typical are the crescent 'c', several stylistic variations on the letter 'W', pseudo-Meissen and Chinese marks. The crown appears after the king's visit in 1788. There are many workmen's marks, and, of course, 'Flight', 'Flight & Barr', 'B.F.B.' and 'F.B.B.' are self-explanatory.

Work Table A table for ladies, at which they did their needlework, etc., made from the second half of the eighteenth century. A lifting top is quite common in such tables; a writing board is often incorporated; a frequent feature is the suspended silk bag or pouch. A different type, the French work table, has a tray for a top and shelves below.

Writing Chair *See* **Roundabout Chair.**

Wrought Iron Ductile iron that has been 'wrought', worked, formed, by hand. As opposed to cast iron, which is hard and brittle, wrought iron is malleable and tough.

Wu Ts'ai (Chinese) 'Five-colour' overglaze decoration on Ming porcelain. The 'five' is misleading as it really means polychrome. Red and green were the main colours used, with the addition of yellow and purple. The *wu ts'ai* wares of the Wan Li period are most esteemed.

Yao (Chinese) Ware—e.g. *Chien-yao*=Chien ware (q.v.).

Yang-ts'ai (Chinese='foreign colours') The Chinese term for *famille rose* enamel decoration.

Yew Very hard wood, reddish-brown, used for veneers in the seventeenth and eighteenth centuries, and in country furniture from the sixteenth century.

Ying Ch'ing ware Porcelain of the Sung (and perhaps the T'ang) dynasty comprising a white or yellowish body and pale blue or greenish transparent glaze. *Ying ch'ing* means 'shadowy blue'.

Yorkshire Chair (also **Derbyshire Chair**) A type of chair associated with these counties, dating from about 1650–75, the back often filled in with two shaped transverse bars.

Yu (Chinese) Ancient bronze wine vessel, cylindrical in shape, with a convex cover and looped handle.

Yüan or Mongol Dynasty (A.D. 1279–1368) *See* **Chinese.**

Yüeh ware Stoneware of the northern celadon type made during the T'ang and Sung dynasties, originally at Yüeh-chou (hence the name) and later at other districts in Chekiang Province. The hard grey body covered by a greyish-green or putty-coloured glaze. Decoration is carved.

Zebra Wood Wood imported from Guiana during the late eighteenth century; light brown with prominent dark brown stripes; used for veneers and cross-banding. It is hard and durable.

Zucchi, Antonio Pietro (1726–95) Venetian painter who accompanied Robert Adam on his Italian tour and worked for him in England at Kenwood, Syon, etc.; was second husband of Angelica Kauffman.

Zürich porcelain Factory founded in 1763 with Adam Spengler as manager. At first soft-paste porcelain was made but by 1765 hard-paste wares were being produced. The factory closed before the end of the century. Zürich figures are greatly esteemed. The mark is the letter 'z' in underglaze blue.